I0104261

# An Inside-Out Revelation

## How Renewing the Mind Will Change Your Life Forever

By

## David R. Cotterill

Grosvenor House
Publishing Limited

All rights reserved
Copyright © David R. Cotterill, 2023

The right of David R. Cotterill to be identified as the author of this
work has been asserted in accordance with Section 78
of the Copyright, Designs and Patents Act 1988

The book cover is copyright to David R. Cotterill

This book is published by
Grosvenor House Publishing Ltd
Link House
140 The Broadway, Tolworth, Surrey, KT6 7HT.
www.grosvenorhousepublishing.co.uk

This book is sold subject to the conditions that it shall not, by way of
trade or otherwise, be lent, resold, hired out or otherwise circulated
without the author's or publisher's prior consent in any form of
binding or cover other than that in which it is published and
without a similar condition including this condition being
imposed on the subsequent purchaser.

A CIP record for this book
is available from the British Library

Paperback ISBN 978-1-80381-591-6
eBook ISBN 978-1-80381-592-3

# Contents

# List of Figures

# Preface

We can live better. We can live differently.

There's a commonly used saying that we are all spiritual beings living a human experience but for most people this means little in practical terms.

To some people it's a nice idea, if a little vague, but it doesn't offer much if millions of people are still living life experiences of mental and emotional unease and confusion, isolation and fear, warring, arguing, hating but still, during all this, searching for meaning and purpose.

In this book I'm not just addressing how to live better, but to function realistically, honestly, and practically as fully human in the two realms of the unseen spiritual and the observed, material realm.

In the material realm we give our attention to the psychological process, by which I mean the body, mind, and the emotions, so I include strategies that will enable us to live better in the day-to-day physical realm.

This is the realm we see and experience with our senses, where we have relationships and jobs, where we gather our personal possessions as measures of success and search for ways to be happy and content, to find meaning, purpose, love, and security. Where we try to impose order on a world that is chaotic, random, and subject to decay and death.

These undeniable realities are symptoms of a deep fracture in the fabric of time, space, and matter so we need to go to the cause of the effects, to the root cause.

If one is standing on the bank of a fast-flowing river watching people float by, being swept along helplessly towards the rapids below, we can try to reach out, to catch their flailing hands, attempting to pull one or two from the water, or we can go upstream and discover what is causing them to be falling into the river in the first place.

For this reason, I go beyond trying to fix the symptoms that manifest in the observed realm to seek out the cause and so I will offer some insights as to how we function in what we call the spiritual realm, because for many people this is the 'other place' and is either of little significance or somewhere to escape to when the physical world gets too tough.

The inside-out revelation brings an end to the illusion of duality because, to function as fully human, we need to see that both realms are one, two aspects of the same existence.

So, I will explain the psychological operating system and the spiritual energy that powers it.

When we align these two aspects of the human experience in practical ways, we have all that we need to function as fully human, not only to live better, but there emerges an option to live forever.

# Introduction

For years I have practised as a psychotherapist, using the traditional skills that I learnt from theories developed in the last century by the likes of Sigmund Freud, Carl Jung, and Carl Rogers.

I qualified as an integrative psychotherapist and became certified in CBT, specialising in stress management, dealing with emotional eating disorders and, as a master-level neuro-linguistic programming (NLP) practitioner, I specialised in fast phobia cures, hypnotherapy, mindfulness, and energy techniques such as EMDR and Havening.

The healing magic was often stunningly effective, for a while, anyway.

My commitment to help people and tenacity to achieve the changes they longed for meant that my clients and I would often meet week after week and most times they would tell me that they felt better, but by the next week they would often find the old patterns of thought and behaviour returning and the cycle would begin again.

Working as a solution-focused therapist meant that my clients often expected quick results and so I rarely had the opportunity to spend enough time with them to explore their deeper issues. Consequently, a lot of the time I was just treating the symptoms because that was what clients asked for. 'Just stop me smoking, stop me drinking!'

So, I did, and they paid me for it.

They stopped smoking, but later, some would report feeling depleted, that they were compensating for their sense of loss, sometimes by overeating (and then having to go to the gym six times a week to ease their guilt) or maybe they would fall victim of another habitual behaviour.

During this time, I was aware that I was one of a growing number of proactive mental health professionals becoming frustrated that, despite advances in methodology, we were still only scratching the surface of human pain.

New theories came and went as we were constantly retraining and learning different skills.

There was always some new magic to try out.

As the clients continued to come and go, awareness of mental health as a societal issue was increasing, and the population was clearly on a downward spiral towards mass dependency on medication, whether prescribed or not.

I was burning out, becoming disillusioned. I completely understood so-called underlying issues, that there were always deeper reasons why people used coping mechanisms, but clients were increasingly looking for fast fixes and the internet was becoming awash with free, easy to access, self-help techniques that ironically were sandwiched between advertising for the very things from which people were trying to gain freedom.

Why was psychological change such a stubborn problem to overcome?

I needed to get to the crux of this. Why were so many people literally unable to change their minds when they wanted to?

## Impossible Dream?

Was this an impossible dream? So much time trying to fix something as important as the human operating system when the system itself seemed to be stubbornly resisting our efforts as if it didn't want to be fixed.

It was like trying to add oil to my car's engine to help it perform better but the car stubbornly refusing to allow me to open the bonnet (or hood, if you prefer).

Why was the system refusing to allow the changes so many people wanted?

Additionally, the media was raising the profile of mental health, reporting that people who had been trying to change their emotional states were even ending their lives in attempts to escape from the pain. What sort of God would create such a system of self-destruction?

Why hasn't nearly two hundred years of psychology found a way of solving this crisis?

The core of the problem must be even more deeply buried than I imagined.

## The Turnaround

Everything changed for me and my practice with the realisation that the entire profession had been barking up the wrong tree.

All this psychology, and the therapeutic techniques it produces, assumes that there is something wrong with the system, something that needs to be put right.

Now I found myself asking a different question: what if there's nothing wrong with the system itself?

What if the problem was more about our lack of understanding as to what the system is designed to do for us?

As I spoke with my professional colleagues about this, from the angle that the system isn't broken but simply misunderstood, I began to find that more of them were following a similar path of enquiry, although many were stubbornly sticking to the something-wrong point of view.

More and more of us were beginning to appreciate that the operating system is perfect and works the way it does for very good reasons.

So it turns out that it's been us, the human operators of this fantastic multidimensional operating system, who have been innocently working under a vital misunderstanding.

**Correcting the Misunderstanding**

Turning the 'map' of the system upside down, I began to see how logically the misunderstanding works.

The system is infinitely creative, but we use that creative function to worry.

It is infinitely imaginative and enables us to run multiple scenarios in our inner space before we even act them out in the world, but we use that function to create anxiety.

The system creates uncomfortable feelings in our bodies if we are preparing to act in a way that could be harmful to our wellbeing, but we call that uncomfortable feeling 'stress' and label it as bad. Then when we medicate, this dampens the effectiveness of the so-called bad feeling and we are in danger of eventually actually preventing it from functioning.

That's like sticking a Post-it note over our car's warning lights because we don't want to know it's warning us there is a problem.

Our operating system will even disable our bodies when we refuse to notice those early warning signs, but we call that function depression.

When we can't take any more pain and think about ending our lives, the system's self-correcting, innate intelligence changes functionality to one that will do everything it can to keep us alive.

When we give up, it heals us.

When we aren't taking notice, it protects us from accidental death, but we dismiss that as coincidence.

It even uses our own internal voice to remind us that we are better than we think we are, that we are limitless, that we are beautiful, that we can achieve more, but we overwrite that voice with preconditioned self-analysis and criticism and shut out the positive.

When it shows us love, we struggle to accept it, often giving that love that is meant for us away to other people.

When it brings us a peaceful moment, we fill that space with activities.

### 'Something Wrong' Psychology

This something-wrong psychology persuades us that we are victims of an unruly mind that resists change, that there are deep unconscious drivers that are harming us, and that we must do something about it.

The something-wrong psychology tells us we somehow need to regain control, but the something-wrong psychology is creating a huge and costly mistake.

The system resists change because it doesn't need to change. It's perfect as it is.

Every consumer item we buy comes with a user's guide. How often do we look at it?

Usually only when there's a problem.

Now we have a problem, and its self-imposed, so I'm pointing us to the user's guide.

It's called wisdom and is available to us all.

## Repent!

When they 'see' that their problem has a potential solution, my clients always immediately ask, 'So what do I have to do now?' They are motivated to start working with their newfound understanding and the freedom it promises. It's both exciting and challenging.

Higher awareness is like getting an upgrade for your device's operating system, shiny and new, so we shouldn't continue to abuse it, but find out what features it offers, take a tour, try it out, take it for a spin!

To get maximum value from our operating system we need first to understand how we have been mishandling it and simply stop doing that.

Repent seems like an old-fashioned word. It's in the Bible, isn't it? Often misquoted as 'Repent, the end is nigh' which maybe conjures up an image of a scruffy tramp carrying a handwritten sign warning of God's wrath.

It doesn't need to be so dramatic. Repent simply means stop and turn around. Walk away from the old way because there is a better way.

## Inside Out

One of the ways we have misused the operating system is by assuming that the source of our problems is external, and circumstances cause us to feel unhappy or stressed or depressed. Under that fundamental misunderstanding it is little wonder the something-wrong industry has grown at the pace it has but with such a lack of success.

The fact that our personal experience of life from one moment to the next comes through the filter of our personal thinking is explained and explored in more detail later in the book through In-perception® and the event cycle.

Once we see this, the leverage for change switches from outside to inside.

Personally, when I began to see the logic in this, that it can only ever work this way and it has only ever worked this way, always, life could not continue to look the same, and using the management system became a fascination rather than a mystery.

This revelation is nothing new, it's always been true, it's just that our habitual conditioning hasn't enabled us to see it, until now.

## Waking Up

Using the operating system to perceive and experience life differently, I began to see how the commercial world has adopted a pattern of creating a problem and then offering a solution.

The food industry sells us addictive food and, on the same shelves, sells dieting aids.

The media presents us with stories which cause pain and then sells advertising space to companies that promote pain relief.

It's very dogged in its mission of holding on to concepts which make a lot of money.

So the continued promotion of a something-wrong model of mental health persuades us that there is a problem and clearly we need something to fix it, something we can't do for ourselves, something outside of us.

We've been persuaded that we are too weak to change ourselves, we need therapists and counsellors and life coaches and mentors.

When we feel bad, we attribute this to external sources, but then we medicate ourselves, take alcohol, drugs, food, gambling, tobacco, internet, any of the coping mechanisms that have been manufactured to suck up our freedom to be fully human; we trade our freedom for dependency on an external object that temporarily seems to ease our pain.

When we wake up to understanding the system is working for us, we can use it naturally to navigate life rather than dampening it down with medication.

## The Cycles and Patterns of Replacement Dependency

If we are in a cycle of dependency, we tend to swap what we think is the external object causing our pain for another external object that promises freedom but then it causes dependency as well.

I call it replacement dependency.

If we look externally for the solution, we are always going to give our power away, and we will slowly die from that dependency.

Our world shrinks, our relationships fail, our careers suffer, and our families are torn apart.

So, after nearly two hundred years of humanistic something-wrong psychology, years of endeavour trying to fix the 'human condition', we find that we've been looking in the wrong direction and that there has always been another way.

## The Innate Principles of the Mind

I discovered that the tools that the operating system provides for us to process and navigate life are invisible, but to get a handle on them, I'll call them 'thought' and 'consciousness' and they operate in a space we call the 'mind'.

As I explored the operating system from a 'nothing to fix' perspective, I was drawn more and more into the present moment rather than blaming the past or worrying about the future. I can't really explain how this happened but maybe it was the freedom from the old mindset of 'something wrong to be fixed' that opened me up to a life lived 'in the moment'.

I discuss the growth and influence of something-wrong psychology later in the book, but dropping all those theories from the past released me to be more creative and adventurous in my life and work.

My inside-out revelation wasn't a new thing, nor was it unique to me. There have been many moments of enlightenment over the years, but none has been pinned down to fact and logic and tend to be thought of as woo-woo and not of practical value but this logical, principles-based aspect of enlightenment has stuck and gained traction and has helped to bring about this shift of perspective in our understanding of the human operating system. For fifty years psychologists and health workers around the world have been correcting the innocent but disastrous outside-in misunderstanding about the mind through practice, research, and many hours of client experiences.

Instead of working from a smorgasbord of over six hundred something-wrong psychological theories, there is now becoming one unified field, one based on principles, one which has opened up two routes to enlightenment, but I believe there is still only one final destination.

The operating system has always worked by these simple principles, the mind is the inner space and within the mind, thoughts arise and we become aware of them. It's then our decision as to whether to act on them or not.

Understanding and using the principles purposefully will restore our operating system to a functionality that no longer creates worry, anxiety, stress, depression, and suicidal thoughts so we can free it up to be more creative.

Secondly, but more importantly, as the patterns and cycles are disrupted, clarity emerges and that clarity will begin to restore the rift between humans and God, our spiritual source.

## How?

Metaphorically speaking, we have had our map upside down. The root of our pain is not out there, it's internal. We must go inside, into the system itself.

At any given moment we are experiencing a blend of the outside world through our senses and the inside world through inner consciousness.

Traditional therapy is often incredibly powerful, specifically if the process helps us to understand the triggers from our past that influence us now, so that they do not adversely affect our real-time lives. In other words, understanding how our inside world interferes with our moment-to-moment interaction with the outside world is one of the major keys to unlocking the changes we need to realise.

So, rather than looking to change our external circumstances, we look to refresh our perception of the outside by changing the effect that our filters have on it.

That is what I call In-perception®.

## Where it all Began

In this book we will benefit from a quick journey back in time to explore, and then restore, two of the most damaging events in the history of human psychology.

The most recent happened about two hundred years ago, the split between psychology and spirituality, between science and church, and that has caused us to become more humanistic and focused on self, brain, and circumstances. That has enforced the outside-in misunderstanding, cutting us off even further from our spiritual sources.

Once we begin that recalibration and align the physical and spiritual, and break free from the something-wrong mentality, we need to go further back to the very source of all this pain, to the dawn of the human era.

But we start with human perception at a horizontal level, on the earthly plane, as we begin to operate properly in relationship to ourselves and others, understanding the operating system via the insights of In-perception® and the event cycle.

This will highlight how improper use of thought creates worry, stress, anxiety, depression, and suicidal motivations, getting our awareness of the unruly mind under some form of control or at least to calm down the emotions arising from overthinking.

Once we are more in alignment with how the system works, we can explore conscious levels, and then move on to getting out of the illusion that we are in our head, restoring the connections to our spiritual source and accessing the power of the creative process more usefully and positively!

# Author's Note

## How This Book is Set out

The message of An Inside-Out Revelation is expressed in two ways in the chapters of this book: psychologically and spiritually.

Rather than being written all at once, this book contains writings from fifteen years of my experience working as a professional psychotherapist, personal development coach, Christian mentor, and psychologist.

Through working with the minds of thousands of people I have distilled one truth: that God is real and active in this world, but I respect the fact that people are always following their individual path to enlightenment, so in these chapters I've explored the two major routes generally used in our society to unearth that truth for ourselves—human and divine.

You can read An Inside-Out Revelation from start to finish or dip into individual chapters and, to an extent, both approaches will work because the revelation is the theme that runs through the entire text.

The first part explores the psychological aspect of the human operating system, the horizonal, physical plane that we experience through our senses.

The second part explores the spiritual aspect of the human experience through the two routes of 'psycho–spirituality', which is human towards God, and 'biblical revelation', which is God towards human.

The third part offers practical strategies to help expand your understanding in the two routes and the different life experiences arising from either one.

My earlier writings have been revised and updated as my experience of working practically in this profession have updated my thinking.

I'm still finding new angles, every moment of every day, that show me how fluid and unpredictable life is and how we humans do our best to impose fast and hard structures so we can feel secure and have some element of control.

We live in an ever-changing spiritual, psychological, and material environment; let's make sure we have our satnav turned on and the settings updated.

This is an unusual book which hasn't been easy to write because it explores different ways to uncover the treasure of the renewed mind, but I hope it will be a treasure map for you to locate and enjoy your destiny.

# Part One

## A Psycho–Spiritual Revelation

*Introduction. We all know there is something seriously wrong with the way we use the creative power of the mind. Millions of people are on medication, addictions are running rife and even for those who manage to avoid drugs, there are countless methods of 'natural' mind-calming techniques being promoted while our traditional mental health services fail to keep up with demand.*

*As we explore the roots of so-called disorders that lead to feelings of isolation, insecurity, fear, and a deep yearning for something other than the experience we are having, we will see how use of the tools that the mind offers us are not understood, and so we misuse them.*

### An Unruly Mind?

However hard we try it seems that there is a part of us that doesn't want to do what we want it to do. There is a battle in the mind to produce the positive, constructive life we want, but we keep falling victim to doubt, confusion, and self-sabotage and so we resort to addictions and medication to dull down our unwelcome feelings of disappointment, guilt, and regret, continually dragging our past around with us like a dead elephant.

Even our most exciting and exhilarating experiences can be overshadowed by memories of a loss or a mistake we made and, to make matters worse, our internal narrative reminds us that if this moment is going well right now, 'it won't last' or 'it'll all go wrong again, just like last time!'

We are often victims of our habitual, conditioned mind and although we can, with effort, change the way we interpret our thoughts, we cannot stop them; they will always be there, in the background. Changes can occur at a psychological level, but we are still only dealing with symptoms of a much deeper problem in the human condition that demands a more radical intervention. An understanding of the root cause will save us a lot of time, money, and frustration.

Albert Einstein is reputed to have said that we cannot solve a problem with the same thinking that created it. We are trying to fix pain with the same system that we use to create it in the first place.

The mind, the human operating system, is a universal model, common to all, and it's how we all make sense of every experience, every event in life, but the way we use it is flawed because we are creating the pain that we want to stop.

The something-wrong psychology of recent times has us seeking outside help to enable us to live in our worlds of stress and anxiety, as we play out our lives in insecurity and fear.

Psychological reframing, and making changes in the way we think, can be life-altering, but change at the deepest level must be about renewing the mind and, without total renewal as our baseline, we will continue to live in the land of loops and repeats.

It's a fact that many people find inner peace in ways that don't directly acknowledge the involvement of God, and similarly there are many who find peace through spiritual practices that are not based on Bible teaching. I will explain how both the psycho–spiritual and biblical routes bring us to a single point of decision concerning our mind's restoration, which can bring about the most beautiful and life-affirming flow of communication between mortal human and divine spirit.

I will also share some practical ways of addressing the root of overthinking that creates these different levels of stress and anxiety, focusing on the fact that everyone experiences life from the inside out, mind first, and that is where changes need to take place.

We will start on the psychological level with a model of the way our operating system processes life's events. I call this the event cycle.

# Chapter One

# The Event Cycle

## Introduction

*This chapter introduces a model of understanding the event processing of the human operating system, which has made a practical difference in the lives of those who realise the potential influence it gives them over their mental and emotional wellbeing.*

*What can seem to be a random and unpredictable process is, in fact, a highly intelligent system that is programmed and conditioned by our deepest motivations, and that's the key—the mind is logical, and it cannot lie or pretend, so understanding and aligning with how it works is an investigation worth undertaking.*

*I will be using two primary illustrative models to help us renew our understanding of the mind: the event cycle and In-perception®.*

*These models explain the 'inside-out' nature of our experience and how we use the gifts of thought and consciousness (awareness) to create our personal interpretation of the outside world from one moment to the next.*

*The event cycle is a diagrammatical representation of the cyclical nature of the mind's moment-to-moment stimulus-response processing, whereas In-perception® explains how every individual is living in their own interpretation of the events through projection of their thoughts and emotional states at any given time.*

## Freedom from Habitual Behaviour

To stop creating worry, stress, and anxiety, we must identify the habitual automatic strategies that we have innocently installed in our mind so that we will recognise them when they reoccur and use the event cycle to practice interrupting the patterns to allow space for fresh perceptions.

At this stage, we are not looking at a different mind, but a better understanding and consequently proper use of the one we already have.

## Independent Operator

We are the operator, not the victim, of our operating system and mastery of the process must be our primary mission and purpose.

A renewed mind operates from a different set of values, so we need to retune our conscious awareness to the alternatives to our habitual thinking.

The refreshed operating system will enable us to operate at a higher level of consciousness, which is vital for us to successfully recalibrate from old mind to new mind.

The event cycle diagram is simply a visible representation of a mostly invisible operating system and, because it operates internally, it's useful to have this metaphorical representation to work with.

We must personally take responsibility for the programmes that run in the mind because we are the only person who experiences them and therefore the only person who can interrupt and change them.

Just like a computer, what we put in the mind is what we get out, one hundred per cent of the time, and like a computer, the cycle runs like a routine and will continue to do so until it is interrupted.

## The Event Cycle

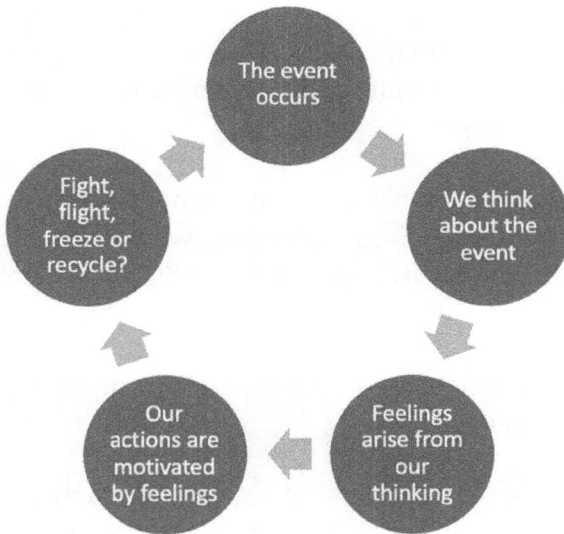

**Figure 1**  The Event Cycle

The event cycle illustrates the way the mind processes our life experiences from one moment to the next. It will help us to understand how our habitual mind's system works so that we can work naturally with the system to achieve renewal.

Any event triggers personal thinking from which feelings arise, motivating us to act. The action might be one of the automatic flight, fight, or freeze responses or a case of repeating, whereby we take our resulting state of mind into the next event, creating a loop unless we interrupt the cycle.

The event cycle shows that, without renewal, we can become innocent victims a closed loop system that causes our experience of life to shrink in ever-decreasing circles of habitual thought and behaviour.

Practices such as those based in meditation and mindfulness stress the importance of us as the 'observer', in other words, as the one that is experiencing the system in operation, but I've discovered that we are more than a passive observer, we are also responsible for programming and running the system, once we realise how it works.

Beyond this cyclic function of the mind is the potential of a greater level of conscious awareness which will enable us to engage with a quality of experience that has no such routines, no limits.

Let's focus for a moment on the impact and implications of us as the observer/operator.

The key is that any event has to pass through our personal thinking, and this means that I will interpret an event differently from another person.

Here are some examples of the way we individually filter events through our personal thinking:

Imagine that you're sitting in your lounge with three friends and a big, hairy spider enters the room, running across the floor in front of you. What would you do? Do your friends act the same way or does one jump up on their chair in fear, another go to stamp on the poor thing, while another reaches out to pick it up?

One spider, four different reactions. Does the spider have the power to beam different responses to each person or is the event of the spider triggering individual thoughts, feelings, and actions?

A second example might be when I go to see a movie with a friend. It's a love story. I've recently ended a love relationship, whereas my young friend hasn't yet experienced true love in their lives. My response is sad, my friend's is passive and disinterested. Again, does the movie have the power to affect our feelings? Not at all, it is an event which stimulates our thinking, in my case my memory, and that in turn creates our different responses.

'Sad film,' I say, whereas my friend says, 'It didn't do much for me.'

When we realise that we are not our thoughts, but we just experience them, and we are not our feelings, but we just experience them, then the misunderstanding that outside events create our feelings must fall away.

## From Inner Thought to Outer Action

Then this is enforced even more if we see how the system also has the innate power to shift from internal to external because it is we who act and that is when the inner system becomes the outer expression—this is the creative process.

To get the best from the event cycle we need to realise that this model reveals a logical aspect of our experience, which I will refer to as 'spiritual' because it is one that happens before form, before the physical expression. It is in this space that we can practice being aware of fresh ideas and inspiration arising from beyond our habitual thinking.

We are not taught this at school, and we are seldom culturally aware of how this aspect of the mind works, so to break the habitual patterns and renew the mind, we need to use this fresh understanding.

Once we really see the observer/operator part of us, then we can achieve a healthy separation from the system itself and we can have more awareness of the mind's operations, and consequently more control over the renewal process.

## Intelligent Principles of the Mind

Within the mind there are specific operational principles at work all the time. These operating principles are always 'on', just like gravity is a power principle that is always on, whether we realise it or not.

We are the observer of our external life events and that is habitually where our primary attention rests, but we can also train ourselves to be the observer of the internal process as well.

The observer/operator uses the principle of consciousness, the gift we have of awareness, the fact that we are self-aware. This principle applies to all creatures to a certain extent, but humans have a higher consciousness, which we need to make more informed choices.

In other words, through the power of consciousness we can observe the external events but also realise how our habitual mind processes them. We can listen to or watch the thoughts arising and be aware of the transition from 'head' to 'body' as feelings arise and motivate us to act.

The observer/operator is the power we use to not only be aware of habitual thoughts arising in our mind but also to think new thoughts, to plan, and use imagination.

This same process includes our ability to feel feelings in the body as the spirituality-based power principle called 'thought' transforms into the physical realm and through feelings emerging in our body. It's these feelings that motivate us to take physical action.

'Thought' is different from 'thinking' by way of the fact that we are aware of thought in our minds, but we use the power of thought to think creatively.

By the gift of consciousness, we are constantly in the creative space between the invisible energy of thought, the transitional energy of feelings and the visible energy of physical action, our behaviour.

## Free Will

We also have what is termed 'free will', which is also shown up by the event cycle model.

There are moments when we can choose which action we take, or to take no action at all, but due to lack of awareness, we often find ourselves acting non-consciously, having to resist powerful, habitual thoughts and behaviours to change our actions to manifest clarity and understanding out of love for others, rather than criticism and judgement out of fear.

In a metaphorical sense, just for clarity, we could compare the human system to that of a car.

To fully function, there are three parts of the car that must work in harmony: the physical body, the internal management system (on-board computer), and the driver.

Similarly, we have a body: we have an on-board management system (the mind), and we are the driver (through the observer/operator). If it all works in harmony, we can successfully get from A to B.

## Brain or Mind?

Another part of the system we must include in any study of the operating system is the brain.

The brain is not the mind, because the brain is part of the physical body, but the mind uses the brain to run the physical part of the system.

Much like a computer (hardware) needs a programme (software), so we often experience our management system making the decisions for us and as a result, the body is operating habitually, taking us in those behavioural patterns, non-conscious actions that we often find ourselves powerless to stop or change. This causes us to erroneously assume the mind is acting independently of our free will, but the system is simply responding to our non-conscious programming.

If we don't steer it, the vehicle takes us where it thinks we might want to go.

If we don't steer our mind, the system will override our complacency and repeat the programming again and again.

Examples of this are emotional eating, drinking, drugs, addictions, repeating difficult relationships, and so on. A lot of this programming took place when we were young and impressionable and runs in the background unchecked and unhindered until we, the driver, take hold of the controls.

## Observer/Operator as Driver

Once we understand how this system works with its operational presets, we realise the power we have as the position of driver and we can override the default conditioning and recalibrate the management system (mind).

We can spend hours in 'talk therapy' but if our habits are chemically imprinted in the brain then talking to hormones has little effect, a bit like trying to remove a screw with a banana.

Generally, when a system goes wrong, the best action is to reset it to the manufacturer's factory settings.

We don't need to take such drastic action because the system hasn't gone wrong. It is the operator who needs retraining, and being better informed will make it easier to work with the system's innate qualities to achieve a much more satisfactory and enjoyable outcome.

The next part explores recalibration using the event cycle.

## Describing the Event Cycle in Detail

The event cycle is illustrative, and I've come up with the design because I like mapping with circles and arrows. The design is not fixed, it could be squares, clouds, thought bubbles, or whatever shape you find useful. The most important aspect is that it is a 'handle' to get a hold of an invisible process, to change the way we use something that is invisible and therefore difficult to grasp with our logical intellect.

So let's start by looking at how the event cycle illustrates the old mind's automatic, triggered responses to stimuli and see if we can identify where, in the cycle, we might be able to interrupt the pattern, cause a bit of useful disruption, and allow fresh thinking.

## The Event

An event is any situation or activity of which we become aware through our senses—what we see, hear, feel, taste and smell.

If the event source is internal, starting with a thought or a feeling, the process is still relevant, but we need to treat it slightly differently because, as it starts in the thoughts, we will habitually try to ascribe that thought/feeling to an external event.

## The Externally Sourced Event

From birth, the way we typically engage with the external world is via the senses. We experience the external world's interplay with the body, the sensations that we feel, the sounds we hear, the sights we see, and the fragrances we smell.

We have all non-consciously learnt to use the senses as our primary source experiencing external events.

As we grow and experience more events, our brain will record what happens and install it in our personal memory, and begin to set up internal templates that will create, over time, our personal internal 'map' of the psychological world.

Examples of such an event in the early years might be meeting another child, parents and carers talking to us in strange voices and funny faces, or our interaction with animals. Then there will be those hurtful events such as falling over or accidents on our bicycle.

Every event is a learning experience and our internal, personal preferences are being set up all the time. We are innocently programming our on-board supercomputer.

These events don't just programme our brain because the brain is just the organisational centre of the entire nervous system. Events are logged in our whole body, our muscles, every cell is being programmed and this will also affect our DNA which, we have recently learnt, changes over time through our experiences.

Falling off our bicycle and hurting our knee at eight years of age will 'scar' us in three places: the brain which records the event, the knee itself that is damaged by the event, and our memory of the event.

That event, unique to us, is one of billions of events that are constantly writing and updating our personal 'script' which we use as our template of how we see the psychological world and make decisions moving forward.

All this activity enforces the impression that life is what happens to us; a series of events that inform and set up our supercomputer to run routines and programmes as we navigate the world.

This enforces our embedding in the material world.

## Our Spiritual Nature

Generally, we are not encouraged during our early years to learn about our spiritual nature.

As a child, we might think that feelings of security and love come from a favourite teddy bear and so our computer/brain will create a template that has us believe that outside objects are the source of our wellbeing.

If we extrapolate that principle through life, then, as we grow, those external objects will become the source of our security, happiness, and wellbeing. The teddy bear, our first bicycle, our friends, our first car, our first love, and so on.

We are constantly giving away the power of our personal, innate wellbeing to these external objects and, as we build up an internal store of needs, a big challenge occurs when these things begin to be taken away from us either through decay, breakages, changes of opinion, or circumstances beyond our control.

If we rely on the outside-in illusion of security, a turning point will come when, instead of gathering new objects, we will begin to lose them and then life becomes one of trying to hold on to things. We then lose the motivation and desire to gain new things in case we lose them too.

Early years events are creating strong patterns of habitual responses, thoughts from which powerful feelings arise and drive us to habitual behaviours that are designed to keep us safe but limit our ability to take risks and rise to fresh challenges.

This problem of habitual programming affects the entire body. We can 'think' about loss but the fear of experiencing it is innate in the habitual mind which is programmed as me first and drives us to gather objects as our security. Gut feelings are a true effect of life events.

Unless we can change and recalibrate our mind, and turn around this outside-in dependency to an inside-out model, our life will constantly be filled with fear of loss and insecurity.

We can enjoy the things of this world when we renew the mind and realise that we can allow ourselves to feel what we call 'bad' feelings because they are part of the system.

Bad feelings can be rooted in innate fears of loss and loneliness but when we try to medicate ourselves to dull down bad feelings, we are just in denial of the full human experience.

A fuller exploration of feelings comes later, so let's focus back on events. Later in life, events can be something as simple as receiving a letter, email, or text. It could be hearing some news directly or indirectly. It could be a chance meeting with someone we like or someone we don't like, either in person or via media.

The event is a stimulus, a trigger for the mind to begin working, starting up our operating system faster than we can normally be aware of.

At a macro level, the event could be a lottery win, an earthquake, or the loss of a loved one, home or job.

At a micro level, it could be stubbing our toe or hearing a joke.

An event is an event, it has no intrinsic meaning, but we as individuals give meaning to it via our personal affections, our previous experience, our values, and beliefs, and these factors all influence our thinking. We give weight to events according to our scripts.

It's never the event itself that is creating the experience, it's the vast memory bank of preprogrammed experiences that are creating our response to the event. This is massively important. I cannot stress enough how important this is to our wellbeing.

Because the process is lightning-fast, it will often seem like the event is creating the feelings, but it never works that way. Our experience is so personal, filtered through habitual thoughts, that everybody literally lives in their separate experience of life.

'There is no such thing as good nor bad but thinking makes it so.' William Shakespeare, Hamlet.

## Thinking

Once triggered or stimulated by an event, our internal operating system uses the power principle of thought to rapidly scan its data banks for relevant information, the primary, personal influencing factors by which we make meaning of the event, giving it emotional weight, before we take any action.

The internal scanning process of the habitual mind is set to the personal defaults, so the mind scans our personal memory banks of experience, and some of the primary search criteria are memories that have strong emotions attached.

However, the search results are based on emotional algorithms which are not chronologically ordered, and so our habitual response to being asked to stand up and make a presentation at work might trigger the memory of a similar previous event at school when we were only eight years of age. How can that be relevant to a fresh event maybe thirty years later?

It's simply that we are experiencing our internal template version of the event, never the event itself.

This is why those four people in a room that we met earlier might respond differently from each other when the spider runs across the floor. The spider does not have the ability to beam instructions to each individual, it's the individual's invisible inner template that motivates behaviour through the event cycle.

That's why you like salad and I don't, why I support West Ham and maybe you don't.

The cycle rarely brings up just the past thoughts into our conscious awareness, but will bring up memories of physical, lived experiences and especially if those experiences were deeply personal, such as affecting our love, our security, self-confidence, etc.

Because the default mind is totally self-focused, it is also protective and interested in our safety and longevity as a physical being, so the search algorithms are set to those preferences.

High level (macro) search results will generally therefore seem 'negative' and that negative bias filters out and informs the micro search which will bring to our awareness memories of relevant experiences so that, preferably, we do not move into action that repeats behaviours that have previously caused us pain or threat.

This is why love relationships are always coloured by previous ones, and relationships with parents and 'first loves lost' are strong influencers.

## The Weight of Thoughts and Feelings

We might experience a different quality to thought depending on the intensity.

Head thoughts tend to pass through our awareness with little impact, whereas thoughts that trigger the whole body's nervous system—those that are feelings-based—are much more likely to capture our attention and motivate us to action.

As an example, if we hear on the news that there is a general shortage of fuel we will take notice, but we will feel more involved in the event if it affects us, such as if our local petrol pumps are empty so we can't get to nursery to pick up the kids.

Our feelings are directly proportionate to the emotional importance and relevance of the event and how we anticipate it will affect our actions/behaviour.

The nature of the energy of 'thought' is that it will remain constant, irrespective of the content of the thinking. It is our personal filters that give weight to the thought. That is why I get more upset if it rains when I've just had my hair done.

For example, I woke up the other morning with two main thoughts in my head. One was that a project that I was involved in had become difficult because of the demands of my employer.

The outcome meant a lot to them personally, they had emotional skin in the game, so my performance as project manager meant more to them than it did to me, and although I cared deeply that I wanted to serve them to the best of my ability, I was aware of the pressure to get it right.

What was the other thought? The other thought was what is called an earworm—Beethoven's Fifth Piano Concerto was playing in my imagination because I had been listening to it before I went to sleep the previous night.

Both 'events' were in my experience through the power of thought; one was emotionally difficult, the other emotionally pleasant, but both intrusive.

These thoughts that we don't think 'on purpose' are what I call sticky thoughts. I could 'hear' my narrative mind chatting away about the problem project to the accompaniment of a majestic Beethoven concerto, but at the same time I could also 'feel' the effects of my thoughts in my body with the result that I was preoccupied, and consequently my ability to give full attention to fresh events that day was adversely affected.

So what did do? I effected the art and science of distraction.

Firstly, I didn't resist the thoughts and feelings because resisting actually involves focus, which means giving attention to that to which I don't want to grant more power.

For example, if I say to you, 'don't think of a pink hippo on a bicycle', you must conjure up the image in your mind before you can 'not' think about it.

Trying not to think about the project kept my attention on the project. I needed distraction, not analysis.

Next, I listened to some different music. That generally overwrites the earworm. Our mind usually retains the last music we have listened to. You might notice that if you turn the radio off during a song, your brain will try to complete the cycle by playing the completed song over and over in your mind for the rest of the day! You might say to yourself, I don't remember listening to that song, but your brain does, and your mind thinks you would like to complete the experience.

## Thinking or 'Thought'?

At this point I need to point out again the difference between thinking and thought.

The ability to think, to have an inner voice, an inner vision, is part of the human operating system and it enables self-awareness and is a vital navigating tool.

'Thinking' is our personal use of this power, this energy which I refer to as a principle, which, like gravity, is always operating whether we believe in it or not.

'Thought' is the term used to describe the power principle and just as the goldfish swims in water but doesn't realise it, we all live in thought and don't realise it, until we do.

My mind is using the principle of thought to play words, pictures, and music in my inner space, and it doesn't care if it's completing 'Hey Jude' or coming up with the solution to my troubled love life. We all give thoughts meaning, but thought is just the event co-ordinator, albeit an incredibly creative one.

What about my other thought-worm, the boss of my latest project? Well, once I could see that the job was more important to him than it was to me, I could see I had a choice to either leave or stay with it. If I left, he would be upset and might blame himself and be under more pressure without me to help him out, so I chose to stay but decided it would be on my terms, working to my comfort zone, not his.

We had a conversation, we were truthful, we carried on. A week later he sacked me.

The event cycle helped me be more aware, to drop into the creative space, re-evaluate, come up with a strategy and carry on.

## Thinking from Beyond our Head

So just to clarify, a fact of our operating system is that we must use thought to access our inner templates and programming, but there's more to it than that.

If we all can think, then we are all using the same energy of thought, and that energy originates from beyond the limited capacity of our little heads.

Once we see the limitless potential of the power of thought, and see beyond our personal programming, we will find that we are also gifted with a system that has innate wellbeing built into it.

That 'other space' beyond the personal patterns has no limits other than those that we impose upon it and if we see that, then then life really opens up, and God or whatever universal power we might believe in comes into play, bringing fresh inspiration from a place beyond the personal patterns, a place even before thought begins.

## The Thought/Feeling Connection

One other point for reflection: Thoughts and feelings can be treated as two sides of the same coin, thoughts being mental and feelings being manifested n the body.

It is because we are unaware of the thought/feeling connection and the part this plays in our perceptual cycle that it will often appear to us as if the feelings are coming directly from the event rather than being filtered through our personal thinking.

It is normally the feelings that motivate us to action. Just thoughts alone are less of a motivator to action, but feelings are a strong motivator, such as fear or attraction.

Depending on our previous life experiences we will each have different responses and this is part of what makes each of us unique in terms of the way we respond to life events and situations, if we only use our personal experiences as the reference for actions.

## Feelings

Here is where we need to correct an innocent but vital misunderstanding about the nature of feelings.

Feelings are like thoughts in transition, manifesting in the body, making the thoughts seem real and alive, dropping from head to heart.

The power principle of consciousness is behind this process.

In God's original design, the visible world was created from the invisible Word. You could say that we are all the result of a divine thought that manifested into a word—let there be light, and there was.

It's like this: thought $\rightarrow$ manifestation (feelings) $\rightarrow$ action.

There is still an illusion at play here that needs some consideration. The illusion is that our feelings are coming directly from an event.

Feelings always come filtered through our thinking. That's what brings us individual perception, interpretation, and action.

For example, if a baby cries, its mother will feel the effect more perhaps than another woman who is also a mother but not a mother of that baby. The more emotional attachment, the deeper the feelings. A single, teenage male will have less emotional connection but if the baby is his little brother, then the feelings will be different again. This innate intelligence built into the system protects both baby and mother.

The relation of feelings to events are always filtered through personal thinking.

We can ask ourselves, what have these feelings got to do with the event? Does the baby have the ability to beam maternal feelings to the mother and annoyance to the teenager?

No, the event is triggering our individual thought processing and that is what is producing the feelings.

You might say that if your partner is upset and you're facing a 'hairdryer' of verbal battering, surely your feelings are coming from them? Never! It just doesn't work that way. Our feelings are never sourced externally, they are never random, they are always personal.

## Attributing Feelings

Another habit, which we innocently pick up over time, is to attribute feelings to events. It's like event cycle in reverse. If I get a nervous feeling, my habitual response is to look outside and see what might be causing that feeling. This way we are creating an event that might not be 'real' as such. This is called projection and I discuss it in more detail later in the chapter about In-perception®.

For now, to keep us on track, I'll use the car metaphor again.

Feelings are like our internal dashboard, but instead of visual they are invisible and internal, and we feel them—they are meant to be alive, not medicated out of action! We don't need coping mechanisms to dull down the intelligence of the system.

Here's another illustration: Imagine sitting in your car, waiting at a red traffic light. There is a car in front of yours, one beside, and another behind. On your dashboard, a warning light appears and a sound indicates that there is only fifty miles worth of fuel remaining.

The question is this: Is that information relating to the car in front of yours, or beside or behind yours? No, it's informing you about the condition of your own car in that moment, potentially motivating you to act and get to a fuel station.

Feelings are informing us of our personal thinking state in any given moment.

Here's another illustration of how convincingly this outside-in misunderstanding can catch us out.

It might appear to us that the sun rises in the east and sets in the west, but we know that's not factually correct. The planet we are standing on moves, the sun doesn't. It's an illusion held in place by a misunderstanding and enforced by popular culture and language.

Similarly, it appears to us that feelings come from outside, from our partner, boss, child, bank account, the price of fish, but it's an illusion held in place by an innocent misunderstanding, enforced by popular culture and language.

We get our power back when we see this.

When I realised that I am the generator of all the feelings, whether I label them good or bad, then everything changed.

It's inside out, it only works one way, ever!

## Good or Bad Feelings

We are designed to be aware of all feelings, so why do we resist what we call 'bad' feelings?

Feelings are thoughts in action, transitioning the creative energy from the imagination into the material world.

We have culturally learnt to avoid what we call bad or uncomfortable feelings.

Medicating unwanted feelings is like covering up your car's dashboard because you don't want to face up to needing to refuel.

Feelings are part of God's design for the human body, an early warning system informing us of the quality of our thinking in any given moment.

However, we need to recalibrate this as part of the renewing process to experience them as internally generated, informative, and useful rather than intrusive.

This again is where we need to be aware of projection. Although, as we've seen, the incoming information is filtered through our personal thinking, there is a double illusion when we then project those filters onto the event.

This can create a loop where we take in external information, process it through our personal filters and then project that conditioned perception onto the external event. We then perceive the event in a different way, giving it a meaning that might be completely inaccurate.

More about this in the chapter about In-perception®, but for now here's a quick illustration of a situation that happened to me.

When I was living in Devon, I used to enjoy taking some time out and driving the short distance from my home to Exmouth seafront. I would walk on the promenade and maybe sit for a while and just engage my senses with the sea and the whole ambience of the place, maybe with a coffee or a Cornetto.

One mid-morning I was sitting by myself on a bench overlooking the beach. There I was, a middle-aged man in a straw hat and shorts, sitting alone and innocently taking time out, not really concentrating on anything in particular.

People on the beach were chatting, walking, laughing together, and several mums were with their children.

In one moment, I caught the eye of one of the young mums and, as her prolonged gaze held my attention, it started up my thinking. My inner voice began to trouble me. What was she thinking? I began to make up a story that she was thinking I was watching her, or worse, watching her children.

My perception changed due to my thinking and consequently my feelings changed, causing me to feel so uncomfortable that I decided that I could not stay there, and I got up and walked away.

I created my own guilt and that changed my perception and consequently I acted out a lie.

## Actions

If we allow the cycle to complete without intervention or interruption, we habitually tend to act out one of the four choices of action illustrated by the event cycle model.

Generally, it's reasonably in context but it's always based on our internal historical habitual templates.

Throughout our lives we are constantly updating our templates; it is a continuous process until the day we depart planet earth, but it's mostly non-conscious.

## Automatic Actions

Depending on the strength of the feelings, our actions could be one of the three automatic survival options of flight, fight, or freeze—what I call the three Fs.

The three Fs operate at various strengths so if we are walking along the road, turn a corner and there is our ex-lover's partner with a knife, we will probably experience our automatic response of fight, flight, or freeze before we have time to think of a different strategy.

Another option is repeat. More on that later.

Once we are aware that the feelings that motivate us to act are internally generated, it should give us some more flexibility in our choices.

However, my experience is that this is not always the case. Certainly, in the early days, and perhaps months, of mind recalibration, I want to reassure you that the habitual drivers will produce cravings, and at times the chemical reactions in your body will scream for attention, demanding that we repeat behaviours that we know are no longer appropriate but 'we just can't help it'.

Talking therapy is great for sharing a problem but talk doesn't persuade hormones to change very quickly; it takes time to change from the inside out, from the thought to the action.

Renewing the mind isn't meant to be a therapy or a cure, it's a renewing. So, rather than teaching you how to change your thinking, we are focusing on the nature of thought, and it is from that higher level of understanding that you will experience new, fresh thinking, perhaps inspired by God's word and spirit as being the way forward to a new life with the new mind.

## Creative Thinking

To help you get out of the repeat cycle, think of it like this: if you bake some cakes and they come out burnt, what can you do?

First choice might be to scrape off the burnt bits and make the best of what's left.

Making a new batch might be a second option but if you've run out of ingredients, that's not viable.

But what if you had a limitless supply of ingredients?

Quite often our options for action arising from an event are limited by our own habitual choices, but God's creativity is endless, unlimited, so if we are tuned into him as our source of love, peace, joy, ideas, inspiration, we can throw away the old 'manna' because he produces a fresh batch every day.

## Inappropriate Action

Next, we look at the way we give meaning to feelings which can lead us to inappropriate action.

The internally generated feeling has no label, no agenda, no personality other than whatever we decide to attach to it.

As I mentioned earlier, it's habitual for us to attribute feeling to an external event, but we can also become obsessed with attributing an unwanted feeling to what we are thinking about, or search our thinking to find out where it's come from.

However, because thoughts are constantly in a state of flux, chasing thought is like chasing a white rabbit that disappears into a rabbit hole, and we get lost down there.

For example, if I wake up feeling tired, I will immediately think about why, thinking about what it is that's made me tired. Maybe a late night, interrupted sleep, a busy day ahead.

We can attribute feelings to internal causes such as mood or worry or external causes such as lack of money, relationship troubles, or worries about the future.

The thing is, feelings aren't aware of anything other than our thinking. Feelings can't see the day ahead or remember yesterday's arguments or last night's cheese and wine.

So if we ignore them, surprisingly, they change, and different feelings arise.

If we habitually give the meaning of anxiety to a particular feeling, we might avoid taking an action that would, in time, benefit us. Similarly, if we attribute excitement to the same feeling, we might rush into an action that, on reflection, turned out to be hasty.

The thought, 'I don't want to go on the roller coaster because it's scary' is a decision based on illogical unknown factors, hearsay, and other people's experience. If, as the observer/operator, we believe our thinking in that moment, we will accept the feelings it produces as true and miss out on the ride.

We've painted a scary picture and run away from our own creation.

So to act based on feelings rather than facts can lead to regret and a hindsight review will have us saying to ourselves we should or should not have done this or that and life would or could have turned out differently.

Knowing how to access your inner space, with time to reflect within the cycle, is the key to taking better, more informed actions.

With a clear, quiet mind, we will be more open to the whisper of the creative spirit rather than the brass band of habitual reactions.

## Reactive or Responsive?

Let's just review the outcome part of the event cycle process.

In the event cycle model, reactive action arising from strong feelings tend to fall into three categories which I call the three Fs (FFF).

F1: Flight. We purposefully withdraw our support or interest in the event, stonewall, refuse to stay in the game (self-protection, habitual mind). We are out of there as fast as a F1 racing car!

F2: Fight. We take on the problem, our innate ego-rebel rises up (habitual mind), we challenge (habitual mind), we criticise (habitual mind), and we judge (habitual mind) the source of the event.

F3: Freeze. Rabbit in the headlights, we don't know what to do. We are overwhelmed with options or just burnt out by the outside-in pressure of trying to please all the people, all the time.

The three Fs are evidence of the habitual mind's limited resources, limited capacity, trying to make perfect cakes from our small batch of stale ingredients.

Then there is a fourth action, which is no action at all, and this means we carry our present state of mind into the next event.

This is recycling an emotional state and can lead to us creating a false reality as we project feelings from a previous event onto the next and so on. This is a loop that may people innocently fall victim to. In order to break the victim pattern, we need to take control of our own event cycle and find a point to interrupt the pattern, jump out, and change our focus.

As an illustration, for a while I used to oversee the running of a team of trades serving housing association tenants. When I was coaching the team to serve our tenants with a more customer-focused mindset, I learnt that it was common for the worker to take their emotional state from one job to the next without taking time to clear their minds between jobs.

Sue was a very conscientious worker but became frustrated one day that procedures—she didn't have a job ticket—wouldn't allow her to fix Mrs Miggins's wonky front gate. In Sue's frustration at 'those stupid rules', she turned up at her next job to fix Mr Jennings's loose toilet seat in a bit of a mood and he, being a military type, reported her for displaying an unacceptably rude attitude towards him and his problem.

Sue had taken the mindset from one event straight into the next. Had she taken time to be aware of the event cycle and break the emotional pattern between jobs, she could have served Mr Jennings with a clear mind rather than with the attitude that got her into trouble. That recycled state of mind was in fact the only link between Mrs Miggins's gate and Mr Jennings's toilet seat.

This is an example of the fourth option that we get caught out with in our habitual mind.

It's the repeat cycle where we skip the three Fs and let the washing machine mind spin from one event to the next, embedding deeper mind-states rather than dropping out and allowing higher conscious levels to bring us peace.

"If you always do what you've always done, you'll always get what you always got". Quote by Henry Ford.

Unless we know that there is another way, we will continue with what we know or what we've done before.

Albert Einstein is attributed to have defined madness as doing the same actions over and over but expecting different results.

That's wisdom for you!

## Changing the Level of Consciousness

Our traditional model of psychology is horizontal. By that I mean that we seek solutions along the plane of understanding that we currently occupy. We metaphorically look to the right and left, ahead and behind, using our personal memories and imagination to create possible solutions. A few years ago, lateral thinking became very popular but using that technique is still generally limited to thinking on the horizontal plane.

An angler might use the same bait for river or sea fishing because that's all they've got in their bait box. By looking around in the greater environment there will be other choices of bait that nature provides, but they doggedly keep on using the bait they believe will catch fish when there is more appropriate bait that God provides through nature. Like manna from heaven, it is more relevant to what we need in the moment.

In a later chapter I will explain about the fresh insights and wisdom available to us all when we move to different levels of conscious awareness.

## Using Psychological Principles to Manage the Event Cycle

We are constantly using the mind's operating principles of thought and consciousness to make sense of events as they happen and most of the time, we are in repeating patterns based on our personal memories—what could be referred to as the first term of reference.

However, thought and consciousness as principles are sourced beyond our personal operating system; they are spiritual, of a divine nature, universal in the sense that they are available for everyone, and everyone uses them.

In origin, the formless principles are fresh every moment, uncontaminated by personal choices, biases, experiences, and conditioning. They are virus-free and available to all of us—and they can provide joined-up answers as well, if we are working on a relationship or in a group.

This provides the options of multiple levels of thought and consciousness and introduces a vertical element to our operating system, where a shift in consciousness enables us to view an entirely different horizon with fresh options.

## The Internally Sourced Event

I want to stress that, although the event cycle is so good at realising the moment-to-moment way the mind processes external experiences, we are all likely many times a day to have internally sourced events that appear to start with the prompt a thought or a feeling, rather than something entering our awareness through our senses.

In these situations, we might have not have 'seen' the event but what is happening is that the innate intelligence of the system is making us aware of something we have missed, via thought and feelings.

An example of this might be a thought arising about a memory or a forthcoming event.

Memories can sometimes keep returning into our awareness and if we have an important event coming up, such as an exam or a difficult meeting, we will be aware of thoughts and feelings reoccurring.

Why does this happen?

If we take the internally sourced event through the cycle, it might be revealed to us.

For example, if internal thoughts about a past relationship reoccur, the next stage of the cycle is feelings—does the thought create feelings or is it staying in your head? If it stays in the head, as it were, it's probably easier to let it pass by. If it kicks off feelings in the body, then you know that the next stage is likely to be the urge to act, which you might want to resist.

We know that resistance gives more power to any thought or feeling (for example, don't think of a pink hippo on a bike! You have to think it before you can 'not' think it), so we can now make an informed decision if we let it pass or act, such as contacting someone to sort out an outstanding issue, or deal with it internally if you don't think it's necessary or helpful to involve others.

It's important to treat an internal event in the same way as an external event because both types of event must be processed by the system in exactly the same way.

As observer/operator we are joining the cycle at a particular point in the process, so, as long as we realise this, we can use the cycle to manage our response to the event.

## Reality or Imagination?

The reason that scary TV programmes affect us is that incoming data is still processed via the event cycle. The system must process ALL events the same way whether they are real or fiction.

Everything is processed the same way, one hundred per cent of the time.

So that's the event cycle. How you use it, how you see it, will be different for everybody so I encourage you to take some time to try it and test it.

'No longer conform to the patterns of the world but be transformed by the renewing of your mind.' New Testament, Romans 12:2.

# Chapter Two

# Pattern Interruption

*'Interrupt the thought, cancel the feeling.' Chris, life mentoring client*

## Introduction

*In chapter one, we explored the event cycle and whenever I've shared this with clients and they have a grasp of the insight it brings, the inevitable question arises: 'This is all very good, but how do I use it to change the way I think?' or 'Yes, I get it, but what do I do with it?'*

*This chapter looks at some ways to interrupt the cycle's habitual conditioning and allow space for fresh thoughts to arise which, in turn, will produce different feelings. This can mean that an event that has habitually produced an action will lose its power, we will perceive it differently with the resulting opportunity to act differently.*

*There will be an element of repeat from chapter one but this is to stress the importance of understanding the event cycle's process.*

## Easy Living?

I'll start with a typical example of the mind's habitual patterns dictating behaviour.

One morning I had decided that I would go food shopping at eleven o'clock in the morning and so in the background of my mind my personal thinking will have already prepared an internal template for this activity, one based on my preference, if you like, my personal map of the world.

This 'map' most likely means that I would go to Sainsbury's, as usual—never Asda—and the chances are that I would probably forget to take my bag for life like I usually did, and I'd probably park in the same space and buy the same stuff, brands I know, food I like. That might sound predictable or boring but it's what I would normally have done.

It was like I was running on tracks!

So, for a different experience, I decided that I'll interrupt the pattern by driving a different route and going to Aldi (shock!). The whole experience didn't 'feel' right and was uncomfortable, but this was me as the observer/operator taking authority over my habits, because, I thought, if I could bust a pattern when simply going shopping, then I'll be more confident that I can bust a pattern that's restricting me in business or relationships and make different decisions generally.

## First Steps

The first step in pattern interruption is to recognise the way our system processes events in the inner space that we call the mind. This process is habitually automatic and, unless interrupted, it occurs one hundred per cent of the time.

We cannot experience our reality without the principles of mind, consciousness, and thought operating in the event cycle because we cannot give meaning to an event without personal thought and the consciousness to be aware of that thought.

In a moment I'd like you to put this book or your device down and engage with the environment around you, allowing a refresh on what the event cycle is and what it does for us.

Firstly, I would encourage you to take a moment to reflect and maybe even create your own diagram of the event cycle, one that works for you and your understanding of the system. Because I'm comfortable with mind-mapping, circles, boxes, and arrows, my default design looks like the one below, but it's understanding the process that's important, not how it's illustrated. The illustration is just a metaphor.

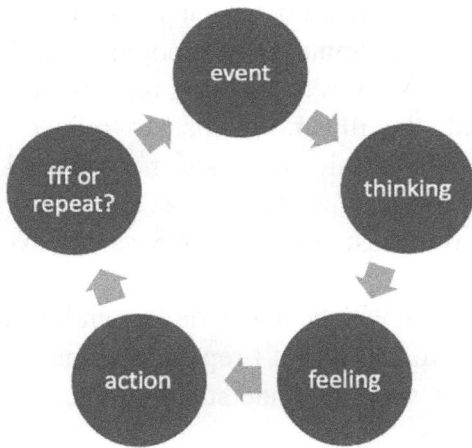

**Figure 2** The Simple Event Cycle

There are four phases that normally run in sequence although the thinking/feeling phase can sometimes seem to interchange. This is due to the fact that feelings manifest from thought and if our thoughts are so habitual that we are unaware of them, then we might experience the feeling first then think about it.

There are four phases leading to action, phase 5.

1. An external or internally sourced event.
2. Thinking about the event.

3. Feelings arising from the thoughts.
4. Action motivated by the feelings.
5. Three Fs or repeat.

A type of this event cycle is used in mindfulness but with more attention to the feeling section, breaking it down into sensations and impulses, but for now it's important to understand that feelings only ever originate from the thinking phase.

If you've created a version of it that works for you, your event cycle might be more formal, maybe computerised, or perhaps it isn't even circular. Whatever the form, remember it is the process that's important. the illustration has to reflect the repeatable nature of the cycle to fully illustrate the potential for recycling and therefore experiencing the next event in the same state of mind that we left the last one, which we want to avoid if possible.

That's the problem with a linear understanding of events and time, as a linear model doesn't repeat, and the repetitive nature of the system is vital to understanding the need for pattern interruption.

## Pattern Interruption

We need to be more focused on our inner space than the external environment to be able to be sensitive enough to identify where we can interrupt the pattern.

The first opportunity for interruption is during or immediately after the event. If we can be aware of our thoughts about the event, we have the power to interrupt before they take hold and manifest as feelings.

We need to recognise our internal commentary that will accompany the moment of the event. It's a voice we will have become used to over time, comforting and persuasive but habitually conditioned to keep us safe, analysing, comparing, judging, categorising.

Practice observing that commentary—perfect it—in order to regain independence from its influence because that voice is there to serve, to provide information, not to be our master.

So we use the event cycle to illustrate the first point of interruption.

It might take some practice to feel comfortable in the observing mode, so practice this with events that are not highly emotional, such as reading emails or activities that are on a to-do list, just to see how they can be managed differently.

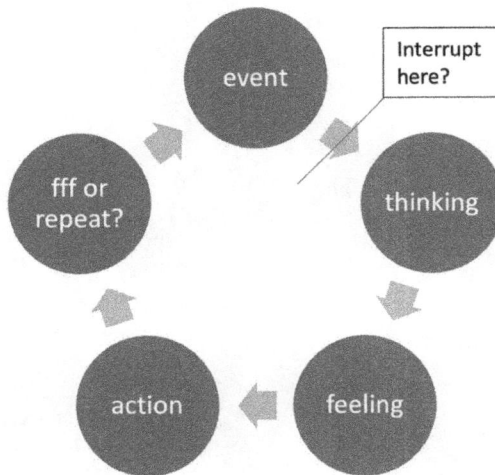

**Figure 3** Event Cycle Pattern Interrupt 1

## Before Thought Begins

Later in the book I'll be suggesting techniques that can help with interrupting the pattern immediately following awareness of an event. I've called these strategies Before Thought Begins (BTB) and Drop it!

BTB is a unique approach to event cycle interruption and with this practice, we can heighten our awareness of the automatic thoughts our mind associates with certain types of events.

This can be useful for observing events without giving them an overlay of meaning, in effect experiencing the purity of an event for what it is without taking our habitual narrative too seriously. This allows the renewed mind to interpret it in a different way, inserting fresh thinking about the event, and consequently enabling us to experience different feelings which will inspire and motivate different actions.

The second opportunity for interruption is in the space after thinking but before the feelings kick in.

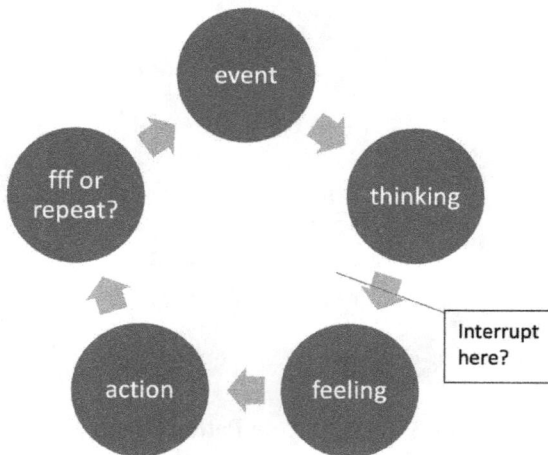

**Figure 4** Event Cycle Pattern Interrupt 2

In a later chapter, I'll explain more about the strategy called Drop it! for pattern interruption between thought and feelings. This is different from interrupting in the space before thought begins. If we can notice that the automatic or habitual thought is creating feelings in the body, maybe because thought has begun the intelligent process of linking memories to thoughts, we can interrupt before we have boarded the 'thought train'.

Once on board the train of thought, we will find comfort in our habitual reactions, experiencing that train taking us to a mental and emotional destination that is irrelevant to the present event because it's linked to an event in our memory. To avoid this, we need to remain on the platform as long as we can and say to the thoughts and feelings as they arrive, 'not this one', and wait for a different one.

Drop it literally means that we drop out of the thought or the feeling through some form of distraction or diversion, and obtain a quiet mind through a meditative practice.

The mind works in context, which means that it will link a present event with a similar experience in our memory automatically. For example, imagine driving along a motorway and seeing a road sign pointing to a nearby town that holds emotional memories for you.

The mind will bring those memories to life in your event cycle even though the trigger has been fleeting. Our attention is drawn away from the road, from the car, and suddenly we are daydreaming!

This is a moment when we must bring our attention back to the present as quickly as possible.

Wait!

The next phase for interruption is before we take any action.

43

Interrupting at this point requires a higher level of awareness but is still achievable with practice.

By this point, habitual thinking will have engaged the consciousness principle and we are experiencing the transition within our operating system from invisible, formless thought to the very edge of visible action, manifestation into the external world of effect.

Our internal narrative drives us with a persuasive motivation to act out what we believe to be true in our thinking, seemingly to be the correct action based on our presets and preferences.

'The Devil made me do it' is an extreme example of being driven to action by an internal narrative created by thought/feeling within the event cycle. At a less extreme level it might just be a gentle nudge but whatever the level of motivational driver, at this point our free will, our choice to manifest via the habitual mind or the renewed mind, is still an option.

## Free Will

Free will is contained within our ability to think whatever we want to before acting. If we are compelled to take actions due to habitual thoughts and feelings based on memory, free will is less obvious.

To wake up to the choice at this point is mastery, you will gain a sense of control and creative energy to manifest different outcomes. To be able to stay in feelings that we know habitually would send us for a fix—our addictive coping strategy—and just watch those feelings dissipate, rather than engage, can be exhilarating, and new thoughts and feelings will arise from this victory.

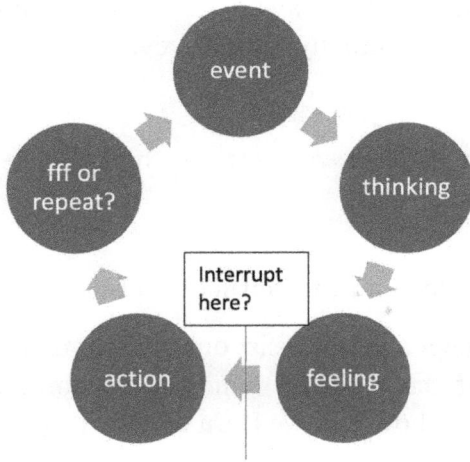

**Figure 5** Event Cycle Pattern Interrupt 3

## A Practice for Interrupting the Event Cycle

This practice has helped for some of my clients and friends.

For starters, just for one day, every two hours, if possible, set your alarm to take a break from whatever you are doing and sit quietly.

As best you can, become aware of your thoughts and see if you can identify the space between each thought. At first you might not even be aware that there is space between the thoughts at all.

This exercise can reveal a deeper awareness of our thinking patterns so I'm not suggesting that you do it for too long—a minute or two, perhaps. Also be aware when you first do this that you will become more conscious of your mind's general activity and the feelings that arise from thoughts.

See if you can identify the stages of the event cycle from an internal perspective.

In this exercise, you'll be aware of events arising inside your mind rather than externally sourced events, but the effect can be similar.

Remember the sequence: event → thinking → feeling (the motivation to act).

## Further Reflections on the Nature of Thought

Learning to accept and not resist our own thinking is vital in the recalibration of the renewed mind. If we don't recognise the habitual thinking, how will we learn to deny its power?

This is why we are not looking at ignoring or denying thoughts. We are watching, to gain authority to be able to shift our state of consciousness and be aware of fresh, inspired thinking coming from beyond our personal database of thoughts.

We are looking to gain understanding, awareness of awareness, awareness of habitual thinking, tendencies to dwell in the past, or worry about the future.

Beyond the personal habitual mind's chatter are different, quieter, inspirational thoughts from the mind's live stream of data, fresh and relevant rather than habitual, conditioned, and stale.

## The Internal Decoder

If a client asks me, 'How do I stop this thought that's constantly in my head?' I would answer that to stop thought would be like trying to stop the blood flowing through your body.

For example, the human heart is called an organ and it pumps blood around our body. It's not invisible, but we cannot normally see it as it needs to be within our body, but we believe that it exists.

Similarly, the brain is an organ that manages our operating system. We cannot see it ourselves, but we believe that it exists.

Think of the mind as an organ, but totally invisible. However, it serves us the same way as our heart and brain.

The mind is 'spiritual' in the sense that it exists in a formless state until we allow the thoughts in our mind to create feelings in our body that might then motivate us to act and bring thoughts to life.

The flow of this system is always outwards. Always inside out.

Event → Thought → Feelings → Action.

It cannot flow backwards.

## Being Online

But the spiritual part of our operating system isn't contained within the body. It depends on information flowing from a greater source, otherwise we would only be repeating the same patterns again and again.

Think of it like being online, connected to the internet of divine guidance, all relevant information and deep wisdom, whereas being offline, all we have access to is what is in our personal database of memories.

When 'online' we can experience fresh thoughts, ideas, and creative concepts beyond our own experience.

Learn to see that within the trap of this repetitive cycle of our personal, individual conditioned thinking there is something else, something greater than our own memories, something very special and something that has the power to interrupt and change the habitual patterns.

Think of our internal system as a bit like a TV decoder. The data flows in from the broadcaster and the TV decoder converts that data into images and sound on the TV screen.

Our smartphone works the same way; the data of the internet is always 'on' but we can't decode it with our minds, we need a phone with a screen and sound.

The intelligent data from the force behind life—I call it God, some call it the universe, whatever you believe in as your source—is always 'on', always broadcasting and our system has a built-in decoder that takes that information and converts it into thoughts that we see and hear and feelings that we feel.

Our operating system is like a software package that receives, decodes, interprets, and projects this information onto the 'screen of the outside world' and that is how our moment-to-moment experience of life occurs.

This steady stream of intelligent information is a bit like the news data tickertape that runs across the foot of the news on our TV screen. Instead, with us, it is flowing through our consciousness and the first time we are aware of it is when we see it in our mind's eye, not with our physical eyes.

This inner vision is always on and where we gain control is realising that we don't have to engage with it all the time. Some of it we just don't want in our experience, and although we don't have control over the flow, we can have control over what we choose to watch, hear, and feel.

## Beyond Personal Thinking

God's gift to us is this mind but an even greater gift is the ability to renew it from the worldly patterns that create stress, anxiety, and fear—a renewed mind that exists beyond our personal thinking.

The renewed mind is tuned into a vast network of information and guidance. The source of this is a bit like a sower pouring out 'seeds' of data, some of which will fall on the stony ground of my disinterest and others on the fertile ground of creativity.

It's our gift of freedom to choose what to focus our attention on, what we want to watch or get involved in.

I'm pretty sure God won't be disappointed if I ignore some of this information, after all, if it's important enough it'll come round again, like those sticky thoughts that keep reminding me that I still haven't paid my phone bill.

## Our Creative Choice

This stream of live data is formless and still generally without meaning or any agenda, until I give it meaning and decide if I want to turn it into form through my actions—introducing it into the event cycle as an alternative option from my limited, personal, habitual mind thinking.

I'm the one giving meaning to the data I'm receiving. To repeat the quote from Shakespeare's *Hamlet*, 'There is no such thing as good or bad, only thinking makes it so.'

Bringing this new thought into being is known as divine ideation, the gift we all have that we can interpret what comes into our consciousness as good or bad or just taking it as it is, without referencing it through our memory.

As mentioned earlier, according to Henry Ford, if we always do what we've always done we'll always get what we've always got. That could be adapted: If we always think what we've always thought, we'll always feel what we've always felt and do what we've always done.

If we innocently assume that we must give close attention to all the data streaming through our consciousness in the form of external data or unsolicited thought, it's no worder we will become stressed, but once we focus in on a particular thought, we give consciousness permission to bring that thought alive by feeling it through to the next state of manifestation—the bodily senses which we call feelings (or emotions—same thing, different words).

Like the expression, 'What happens in Vegas stays in Vegas', what happens in the mind can stay in the mind until we decide to bring it to life, and it flows into the body, through which it must then flow out of, to manifest in the external world.

## Projection

Our operating system is more like a movie projector than a camera.

Thought is the film, consciousness is the light bulb, and our mind creates the screen upon which we project our 'movie', like a 3D, interactive event.

We are the creators of the personal world we step into from one moment to the next.

It will always appear to be same movie until we interrupt the pattern and allow a different reality to manifest.

I call this process In-perception® and more about this later.

# Chapter Three

# The Overthinking Progression

*'If overthinking burnt calories, I'd be a supermodel.' Anonymous.*

## Introduction

*I wrote this chapter when I realised there was a need to understand how any prevailing state of mind, such as positive and optimistic, or sad and pessimistic, will affect the way we interact with the event cycle, leading to a deeper understanding of the constantly fluctuating state of thought and feelings within the mind. It will be best to read chapters one and two before dipping into this one, but it can stand alone and will be useful if you are feeling overwhelmed.*

## Worry

We all worry, it's part of life and let's face it, we usually just get on with it.

Worry is a common way of describing obsessively thinking about an issue that needs a solution, but we don't have a clear idea what to do for the best, or a potential solution seems beyond our control.

In other words, we set our minds on an issue, we have no solution and so we feel out of control and, because our mind is creative by design, it will set about attempting to pull together potential solution options to offer us, usually by using our previous life experiences (memory) as the source of these options.

This is all very well, but if our previous life experience has no relevant solution, or if we still don't have enough information to resolve the issue, then we will continue to worry.

The worry progression can be temporarily avoided if we are distracted, and then we will forget that we are worrying until we are aware once more that what we were worrying about is still unresolved and it starts again! It's like having a headache and then realising that the headache has gone without noticing the moment the pain stopped.

This creative process is an indication of the intelligent nature of the mind and the way the principles of thought and consciousness enable us to be aware of both external and internal activity. Both are involved in the process of decision-making at each moment in time.

**Life as a Journey or a Series of Events?**

Some people see life as a journey, everything linked in a path to an end somewhere, whereas others, at the other end of the spectrum, see life as a separated series of events, challenges to be overcome before moving on to the next one.

It's worth spending a little time reflecting on our personal preferences, how we have come to see life through our habitual programming and if we would benefit from an alternative viewpoint.

For the person whose life is one event after another, the worry and stress of creativity might be easier to cope with if they were to pause for reflection as they completed each cycle of activity.

The brain chemical dopamine has a lot to do with this. Completion gives us a happy feeling and so seeing life as a series of events that need completion for us to feel ok can lead to a series of chemical highs (completion) and lows (disappointment).

If we see life as a journey, then we might be more stable emotionally but stress might build along the way and if we have no completions at all, we can get bogged down.

Chronic worry can be stressful as long-term or multiple worries can lead to an underlying tension in the body, commonly called anxiety, a sort of background feeling of unrest or impending doom.

Too much of this overthinking and anxiety will start to cause our operating system to falter, almost like it has a virus, and we will feel tired, overstretched, irritable, or worse.

The more anxious we become, the less tolerance we have, and we can become snappy, irritable, and closed off from others.

If we continue to stay in this state, depression can result as the energy we need for thinking is rerouted into our nervous system and shutdown becomes a distinct possibility.

Another result arising from such worry is avoidance, through deadening or preoccupying the mind with avoidance strategies such as alcohol, drugs, internet, etc. We all have a preferred medication, stored in the medicine cabinet of our mind, be it prescribed or not!

If not checked, our overthinking can result in a mental health progression like this:

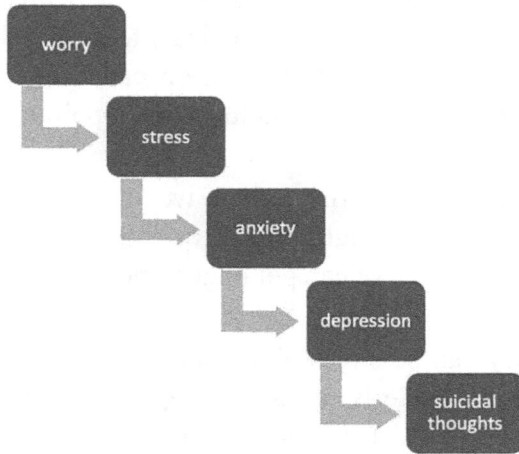

**Figure 6** The Overthinking Progression

This overthinking progression is another illustrative tool we have that illuminates the mind's tendency for habitual overthinking, which is a progression that feeds on itself.

The elements of the overthinking progression are:

Worry, an activity; it is active overthinking.
Stress is an emotional state arising from overthinking.

Anxiety is a deeper emotional state that affects our tolerance levels and introduces an underlying sense of fear or dread.

Depression is where the system is severely overloaded and begins to shut down to protect us from more fear. We may become isolated from the environment, friends, and family, becoming more and more self-absorbed.

Suicidal thoughts arise as the system shifts from shutdown to hyper awareness and although we might still be seeking a way to escape from fear (such as when we attempt self-destruction), the system's innate benevolence and self-care will now shift to survival mode.

Suicidal thoughts are not yet 'acts' but if there is intellectual planning about a method of self-destruction then external intervention might be needed.

I'm not in any way suggesting that worry will inevitably lead to suicidal thinking but I'm using this as an example of how worry sits beneath our conscious awareness. It has the potential to expand to more serious unhelpful patterns that will inevitably produce unwanted and uncomfortable thoughts and feelings that in turn will colour our view of the world, affecting our state of mind and emotional health.

To break the pattern, we can use the principles of the mind to shift into the higher state of consciousness that is observing the process rather than being a victim within it.

What I'm pointing to again here is the common denominator in this process—our thinking.

We can use the event cycle model to gain an understanding of how we innocently allow the principles of thought and consciousness to create our personal worry, stress, and anxiety in our mind.

Worry is an activity (overthinking), whereas stress, anxiety, and depression are states arising from the activity but still maintained via thought, and the final element in this overthinking chain of events is suicidal thinking.

The potential of self-destruction is not often acted out because in most cases our system, although oriented for peace and quiet, is fundamentally all about survival.

As the system progressively shuts down to survive the stress of overthinking, it will most times protect us from actions that are unhealthy or life-threatening.

This is part of the beautiful, innate wellbeing that is built into the system, and once we are aware of it, we can trust it more and better get to know its strategies.

So how can we step into this overthinking progression and stop it progressing from one stage to the next?

## The Seductive Power of Thought-in-the-Moment

*"Our bodies are the texts that carry the memories and therefore remembering is no less than reincarnation" Blessel Van Der Kolk, Psychiatrist.*

We can be aware of many thoughts simultaneously and although we can only focus on one thought at a time that one thought contains the creative power to influence our in-the-moment experience.

The principle of consciousness empowers thoughts, transforming head-thoughts into an embodied emotion. Embodying any of our own thoughts, outrageous as it might sound, influences the way we perceive the outside world.

To realise that our moment-to-moment experience of reality is shaped by thought-in-the-moment in this way can be both shocking and enlightening.

Due to the fleeting and subjective nature of thought, a fresh thought will come along at any time so although in one moment we might be overwhelmed by a thought about a traumatic past event, we can regain our equilibrium when we realise that we have freedom to choose the next thought to cultivate.

Thought-in-the-moment is an ever-changing transitory experience but it can be immensely creative in the way it shapes our perception from one moment to the next.

# Chapter Four

## Conscious Levels

*'No problem can be solved from the same level of consciousness that created it.' Albert Einstein.*

### Introduction

*One of the principles operating in the mind is referred to as consciousness and this is the mind's ability to make our thoughts appear so real to us that all other realities vanish, and we are absorbed with whatever we are experiencing.*

*We assume all that exists is what we can see around us, and we can forget that there are higher and lower states of consciousness available to us at any moment. Within these states are various world views which means we can be in a situation that, depending on our conscious state, could vary as an experience from ecstatic to boring to downright depressing.*

*However, it's not just about our state of mind. What can also happen is that, at any given moment, our feelings influence our experience. We find that mood shifts for no logical reason and what might be a difficult task in one moment becomes fun the next. This chapter goes some way to explore this phenomenon.*

### The Me-First Mind State

The personal, me-first mind is only one relatively small aspect of the total operating system we have at our disposal and if we stay in a locally focused conscious state we will see limited options. Universally, the levels of awareness or consciousness are unlimited, so when we are in a higher state, the mind offers unlimited options of alternative perceptions of any given situation.

There are seven billion people on planet earth, each with their own personal thought systems, so which person has the correct interpretation of any situation?

Seven billion alternative realities and each one seems the right one for each individual, even though these states are subject to constant fluctuation.

## How Misuse of the Principles Creates Stress

Let's have a closer look at the implications of the principles understanding with regards to worry, stress, anxiety, depression, and suicidal thoughts using the event cycle and the overthinking progression as our models.

Of the principles, 'thought' is the more obvious common denominator in the overthinking progression model.

As a cultural society we have been working on a misunderstanding that the mind works independently of our consciousness and so we can be easily persuaded by the power of thought that we are worried, stressed, anxious, depressed, or suicidal.

It is not a new expression in coaching/therapy circles to say that 'we' are not our mind. It's been a part of the agreed mental model for many years that we have a mind but few people I've worked with benefit from the understanding of what mind really is and how to use it to our advantage!

'Mind' is another word to describe our psychological human operating system and within it are the practical and immeasurably powerful energies of thought and consciousness.

As individuals we use these principles to experience our world but we each use them differently, depending on our state of mind at any given time and other, longer-term influences such as previous life experiences, background, culture, and education.

The principles are invisible to our five senses because they are fundamental elements that existed before the formulation of our personal experience, but they interact with our senses to create our experience. So the event cycle (see chapter one) is a basic illustrative model to give a visual aid to understanding an invisible process and the overthinking progression can help us to navigate the feelings and emotions that try to drive our behaviour.

By making the process visible, albeit metaphorically, we can more easily interrupt the patterns that are unhelpful and change our perceptions of moment-to-moment reality as it appears to us.

## Different Levels of Consciousness

Habitually, at what we could call a default level of operating consciousness, we are aware of what our senses are receiving mixed with our internal thoughts, impressions, images, and the internal narrative. This is what I call the horizontal plane.

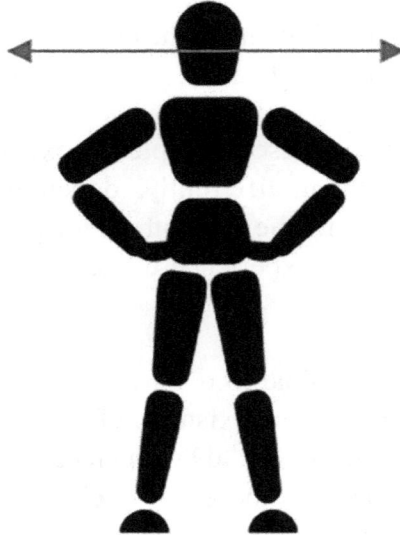

**Figure 7** Conscious Levels Horizontal Plane

In the illustrative drawing of the horizontal plane, we are limited to what we know by personal experience (memory) or imaginations about what might happen in the future using the past as a reference.

It's a bit like only having access to the hard drive memory of a computer without being connected to the internet.

Once we are online, we have access to millions of options rather than just to those limited to our personal experience.

If we drop the idea that the mind is limited to being attached to the brain, then we could see the mind as spiritual, non-local, with intelligent information for us to use. It's like in-game guidance direct from creation itself, flowing from the source of life, so let's see how to access it.

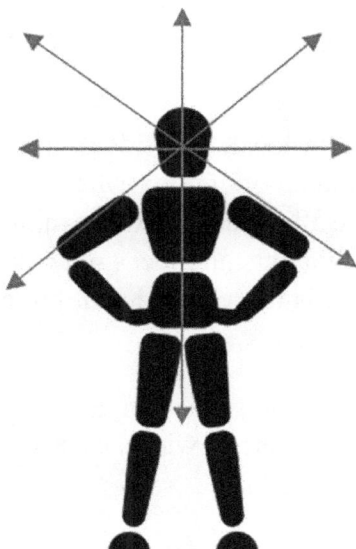

**Figure 8** Conscious Levels Multiple Planes

In this second illustration, we have multiple options through our personal mind's connection to the universal source of intelligent consciousness (God or the universe) which is enabling us to access more conscious levels and more options. More like being online, connected to the unlimited levels of guidance and information. This way we are able to access higher states of information even if we are in a lower conscious state.

I accept that not everyone finds it easy to consider a universal divine intelligence, let alone one that has relevant information to us personally for our day-to-day living, but this is where I ask you to suspend everything you thought you knew and try it for yourself. Please don't just take my word for it, this is a personal experience.

The truth is that if 'spirit' or 'invisible power' or 'universal energy' is sourced beyond the individual human brain, this must influence our view of life because if this revelation is missing from the operating model, then mind will always be a mystery as well as being extremely limited.

Put simply, if mind is local, individual, assumed to be 'in our head', then we will keep on getting what we've always got. But then, surely don't we all experience those moments of inspiration, when we get fresh thoughts and ideas out of nowhere, and could this be because mind is more than local, but a multidimensional 'life source' beyond ourselves?

Whereas the individual personal human brain is temporal, time-based and primarily concerned with the senses, mind is unlimited and connected to all potential.

Therefore, in this operating model, the mind is spiritual, formless, and the brain is the primary part of the physical body, which manifests thought into consciousness and actions in the world.

Enlightenment really does begin with this inside-out revelation.

## Enlightened Mind

Personally, finding that the universal divine intelligence which we call mind was the key to understanding what it means to be fully human, and everything changed.

I was no longer 'in my head' with a limited life and I finally understood why I can 'see' images, hear voices, and feel feelings that are not coming outside in through my eyes or ears.

I realised I am connected to a greater source. A greater space that I had been innocently assuming was 'in my head', and connected to a flow of creative, intelligent energy that is unlimited in the ideas it can show me.

So it's to this space that I go when I want to interrupt the pattern of worry, stress, anxiety, and depression, because I can expect the unexpected to flow into my mind, once it's quietened down and I've jumped out of the event cycle loop.

At personal level we become innocently conditioned to see life horizontally, on a plane of perception. 'Look around you, what do you see' tends to be our options. As a quantum principle, mind is showing us universal conscious levels, within which we can see multiple options.

## Seeing the Bigger Picture

As an illustration of how conscious levels enable us to see the bigger picture, I often recall an experience I had in London a few years ago.

A few friends and I had received invitations to the opening of a new club in London that was situated on the roof of an office block opposite St Paul's Cathedral.

On a warm summer evening we arrived at the venue to find what seemed like an overwhelming number of young people crowded around a small, external, glass-fronted elevator that held about six people at a time. We had VIP passes so we pushed through to the front of the crowd and entered the lift. As the doors closed, although we could see the crowds, the sound of their chatter and laughter ceased and we began to rise.

The higher the elevator travelled, the more I anticipated the outcome.The crowds were left far below, and we emerged above the rooftops into a clear blue evening sky and a magnificent view of the cathedral and surrounding buildings.

I experienced different feelings the higher we went. The view was better.

Here's another illustration: Imagine you have a house where the kitchen is at the back, overlooking the garden. Having recently moved in you haven't had time to clear the overgrown garden and every time you look out of the ground floor window you see the garden and have anxious thoughts about it, when will you get time to do it, what will the neighbours think, when might you be able to invite friends round to sit in the garden, and so on.

But when you go upstairs and look out of the bedroom window, you see beyond your personal garden into the neighbouring gardens and the scene is different. You see that there are other gardens in a worse state than yours but there are also gardens that are neat and tidy.

Perhaps seeing this, you can  relax, once you see the bigger picture and realise that the pressure is all your own.

The bigger picture can act like a reboot. We don't always need to drop back to the start of each event process to find the space before thinking begins. We can drop out of the personal perception at any stage.

## Conscious Levels, the Overthinking Progression, and the Event Cycle

When overwhelmed, we tend to innocently (but incorrectly) believe that events are conspiring against us.

However, if we see each event as separate, as just one in a series of events, this breaks down the effects of the thought/feeling cycle and, with practice, we will start to see the point where thoughts about any given event begin to arise.

By seeing that it is thought that is always creating our feelings, not the event itself, we regain control and, with practice, develop a margin of separation from the personal mind's habitual responses, allowing the universal mind space to intervene with alternatives.

The event cycle model gives us some options to visualise an invisible process, aimed to give us some control or power that works with the system rather than against it.

What we also need to be conscious of is where we are at any given moment on the overthinking spectrum which will influence or colour our state of mind. In other words, if we are worrying about multiple future events we will not be paying as much attention to our options in the present moment when current live events arise.

If we are stressed, we will have less tolerance and be more occupied with our inner world, less conscious of our surroundings; if we are anxious, we will be snappy and irritable.

Reflect on this again now. I'm sure we have all worried at some time. I'm sure we have all been stressed, anxious, depressed, and even had suicidal thoughts sometimes. Even though our thoughts might not be 'bad', but just carry a desire to escape to a tropical island, that's still a desire to remove ourselves from a present-time situation or a lifestyle that we can't cope with anymore.

So, as we move along the overthinking spectrum, our tolerance levels drop and our ability to take on more information, tasks, or activities drops proportionately, and we become more and more focused on our inner world.

We can observe this in family or friends when they become more anxious, they drop out of social events, don't return our calls and, as depression takes over, become more self-absorbed and reclusive.

If we can understand this process, it will help us be more understanding, less demanding, and less likely to tell friends to 'man up' or 'get their act together'.

## Working Conscious Levels

If we can see when we are stuck on a me-first horizontal plane of consciousness we have the option to wake up to that moment and see the situation from a different level of awareness.

We know as a fact that everyone has the ability to see any given situation differently, from their own perspective, so the only way we can be fixed at a particular conscious level is through our own innocent ignorance.

Practice interrupting the event cycle and using the creative power of the mind to shift to a higher conscious level.

Maybe ask yourself, how would Einstein work this event?

How would your favourite superhero work the event?

By contrast, how would a person whose eyesight is limited work the event?

Use that amazing ability that we call the imagination to run movies in the mind to 'see' different perspectives and doing this will automatically shift us to different levels.

## The Inside-Out Experience

Let's regroup now and reflect on this inside-out revelation of our operating system.

The principle of thought is always on, like gravity; we cannot turn it off, so we might as well get used to it. Live with it. Don't avoid it. Don't resist it. It is our psychological and spiritual lifeblood.

Our part is to recognise the gift of thought, be selective in our attention to the specifics that are relevant to us and let the rest go by.

If you're on the railway platform waiting for a train to London, you don't get on every train that stops, do you? You watch the not-this-one trains go by until the one that's right for you arrives, and then you get on that one, knowing it will take you to your chosen destination.

Maybe the correct thought train for this part of your journey will arrive at a different platform, the one a little higher up than the one which you currently occupy?

Thinking is how we can describe our personal use of the principle of thought.

Being aware of our thoughts and feelings is our personal use of the principle of consciousness.

Thinking is what we do, we are thinking creatures.

Ask a goldfish, 'How is the water?' and if it could reply, it might say, 'What water?'

It's like that with the principle of thought, we are in it, we exist in it, it's always on.

Awareness (consciousness) is what we are; awake with free will to feel the reality of our thinking as it materialises through us and into the outside world.

The system works innately, instinctively, but can we enjoy the innate wellbeing that's inherent in this system with all the worry, anxiety, and stress of our everyday lives?

Can we really begin to appreciate that negative thinking is equally as creative as positive thinking, because then we will be less judgemental and be infinitely more creative and productive people.

Let's see that every event is a stimulus to begin the event cycle process and that, any time we recognise when we are listening to our me-first self, we have the option to use universal consciousness or spirit to shift our perception and open us up to unlimited different options.

**Awareness of the Cycle**

Let's just recap the way we become aware of each event.

The external event enters our consciousness, through our senses, into the body/mind and microseconds afterwards engages our thinking, and we automatically begin to run it through our personal memory bank to give it meaning.

Faster than we can purposely think, our mind's creative problem-solving process kicks in, sorting, comparing, reasoning, and produces results in a time that Google can only dream of.

It's as if we are served up with our mind's best option for us, one that our mind considers to be the safest, most probable response comes into our consciousness and the body's chemistry kicks in, producing desires to motivate action.

The action is often based on previous experiences (what I call our preferences, script, or schema) and this is where we find ourselves caught in a loop. Even if we desperately want to try something different, quite often, no matter how hard we try, we find the system overrides our desires.

## Using Conscious Levels to Interrupt Habits

So I hope this part has helped to expose the old mind's strategies and enabled you to see where you can begin to make practical changes to recalibrate to the renewed mind.

Test this for yourself. Reflect on the event cycle and the overthinking progression and see if you can open to different experiences from moment to moment.

As I mentioned earlier, at the time of writing this there are about seven billion people inhabiting planet earth.

Which one person has got it right?

Who is using the model that is the maker's design?

## Working with a Principles-Based Coach/Mentor

What is principles-based living and how does a principles-based psychotherapist, life mentor or coach operate?

Put simply, coaching and mentoring is getting more out of yourself than you can get on your own. Principles mentoring is not a theory, or another set of techniques, but an understanding of how our psychological and spiritual experience is created from the inside out from moment to moment.

Life coaching has become a popular alternative to counselling as it is perceived to be more proactive, with less attention on trying to fix something that has gone wrong, or trying to overcome limitations from our past. A principles approach begins with working from a starting position of a functionable, innate operating system that become corrupted through a misunderstanding of how it works and incorrect use.

I can confirm by experience. As a psychotherapist who has worked with hundreds of people, in my experience, no one needs to be 'fixed', and no one can factually be limited by their past, especially with regards to what they are doing in the present.

However, through an innocent misunderstanding of the power of thought in what we call the imagination, we can bring thoughts about the past into our present experience and thus contaminate what is now.

Having said that, we are all often influenced in the present moment by our lived past experiences playing out in our mind. This can be debilitating and leads to many different psychological disorders that carry various labels in the world of traditional psychology.

Ok, as humans in a complicated and unpredictable world we do get stuck, we do get insecure, and we can feel like we lose control, and ultimately we forget to live life fully.

However, I believe there is a different way to achieve life's changes with common sense and wisdom being the keys to ultimate mental health and these are always available to us because they are part of our 'default setting'.

The thing is, as we grow through the early years of life, we can just get too conditioned into functioning primarily with our analytical and critical thinking and, as a result, we lose touch with our inner wisdom, intuition, and common sense.

In the meantime, we acquire a lot of negative beliefs about ourselves, other people, and life in general; this profoundly affects our wellbeing.

We forget that living with wisdom, intuition, and common sense is how God, through the nature of creation, intended for us to function—and we are part of nature, not separate from it, but we also have a mandate to care for it.

Our mental functioning influences every aspect of our lives daily.

The good news is that the more you understand the principles behind the experience of life, the more it increases your power. and you become a lot more secure.

The more secure you feel, the more you stop living at the mercy of external factors, and life does not look so threatening anymore.

The benefits derived from principles-based coaching include drastic reduction of stress and feeling at peace with life in general.

My clients have experienced depression and anxiety-related problems fading away, their confidence and sense of wellbeing increasing, and their relationships transforming.

They find new inspiration at work or discover the courage to make changes or even rebuild their careers from scratch, based on a foundation of clarity, fulfilment, and ease, instead of being driven by fears and insecurities.

Understanding the principles and applying them in your life can:

Lift the effects of depression.
Disperse stress.
Relax feelings of anxiety.
Disperse effects of panic attacks.
Overcome fears and phobias.
Increase confidence/self-esteem.
Help to understand roots of weight issues.
Overcome insomnia.

Increase motivation.
Give confidence for public speaking.
Unlock creative blocks.
Be great for executive coaching.
Be brilliant for business coaching.
Increase productivity.
Inspire leadership creativity.
Enhance or heal relationships.
Enhance communication.

# Chapter Five

## In-perception®

### Introduction

*In 2009 after my first few years practicing as a hypnotherapist, I decided to write my own book using the understanding I'd gained and the techniques I'd learnt. It was called* Stress Reprogrammed *because my specialism was helping clients to understand and overcome stress, anxiety, and fear in their lives.*

*What follows in this chapter is the first update to* Stress Reprogrammed *that was published in 2013. It sets out a deeper understanding of the mind's function and continues my passion to guide people to be their own agents for change with life coaching. It also brings an awareness to more of my clients of how the principles of thought and consciousness work so we can all wake up from our habitual thought systems and find fresh ways of thinking, feeling, and acting.*

*My first book used the field of psychology called NLP but over time I found this was limited to a more humanistic, horizontal-plane model and, as a more spiritual operator, I needed to find more depth.*

*In this chapter I reveal the operational strategy called In-perception® showing how to purposefully engage in the function of thinking as the most influential part of the human operating system.*

*Inspired by the effectiveness of this strategy I trademarked In-perception® as the term that identifies the way the principles of the mind are always operating the inside-out, mind-first nature of our human experience.*

*This is still primarily humanistic and psychological but as we begin to use it to interrupt the worldly patterns programmed in our mind, spirit will begin to lead us into a greater realm.*

*No need for therapy?*

*Could it be true that if we understand how the operating system works and use it properly, that there is no need for traditional therapy?*

## Why In-perception®?

In 2009, when I started to write *Stress Reprogrammed*, I was qualifying as an integrative psychotherapist and hypnotherapist to add to my license as a practitioner in NLP. I regarded these modalities as positive, action-oriented approaches that help people overcome their problems and enjoy a life of freedom and success.

During 2010 I came across a new understanding in spirituality-based psychology that was taking the world of coaching and therapy by storm, and I started coaching clients in this understanding with success. Since then, I have studied in this field and become qualified as a practitioner, coach, and mentor.

This chapter is an exposition of my findings as part of my continuing discovery into how our experience of life is created so we can live it the best way we can.

Principles-based psychology is a new, single paradigm in understanding the spiritual nature of the mind and, put simply, states that we create our experience of life from the inside out.

In other words, the mind doesn't work like a camera, recording what is outside of us, but rather that the mind is like a projector that uses the power of thought to form our personal experience from moment to moment.

## How the Principles Operate

Thoughts and feelings are effectively two sides of the same coin, and although sometimes feelings seem to arise without thinking, they are just thoughts that haven't formed into internal images or internal dialogue.

A thought is metaphorically speaking 'in the head', whereas feeling is the energy of thought manifesting in the body.

When a feeling seems to be instantaneous to an external event, it might seem to be caused by that event, something outside of us, but no, feelings are thoughts, deep thoughts, but still thoughts so we are always feeling thought taking form moment to moment—one hundred per cent of the time. That's how the system works.

We see/hear/smell/taste/touch with the senses, we think, we feel, we react (often this seems to happen simultaneously rather than sequentially).

Seeing/hearing/smelling/tasting/touching do not cause the reaction or response, thinking drives our experience.

The stimulus does not create the reaction. It appears that way, just as the sun appears to go round the earth but it doesn't, and just as an echo sounds as if it comes from another place, the experience and the feelings always originates inside us. What appear to be the things that cause our feelings are in fact just like echoes, reflections of our mind's operations.

Physicist David Bohm is reported to have said, 'Thought creates our reality and then says I didn't do it!'

Feelings themselves cannot exist without the thought as the generator.

Your thinking, not the external stimulus, causes the emotional response (brain releasing activating chemicals into the nervous system), which then can lead to action or 'behaviour'. See the event cycle in chapter one to illustrate this further.

## In-perception® in Action

This revelation of the inside-out nature of experience motivated me to work on the title In-perception®, which I trademarked in 2014.

We perceive what is in the external environment from inside our mind and the mind filters what we 'see' outside according to our state of mind at any given time.

In other words, we observe an external object, and that object is totally innocent of our observation, but when we project a thought onto it, the object takes on a personal meaning to us. Then our internal commentary starts up and it seems to us that it's the object that is making us feel a certain way.

Consequently, the object now has meaning attached to it and we then have a fresh and different thought about the object, which is now overlaid by our new personal meaning.

Our brain processes the new meaning we have given to the object, referencing our previous experiences and according to our preferences, cultural biases, lessons learnt, etc., the object appears now to reflect back to us another new meaning, but it's just another 'echo' of our projections.

We now perceive the previously neutral object as having new meaning.

The loop continues as we reference the rebranded object and project a revised meaning onto it and the echo effect is made stronger.

This can continue and create a perception loop that feeds upon itself.

An example of this might be if you see a car in the street. The car itself has no way of projecting feelings. Ok, it's designed to look great and therefore appeal to potential buyers but it does not intrinsically possess the ability to project 'buy me' or 'desire me' emotions, it's the human that projects those thoughts and feelings onto the car, depending, of course, if the human has their preferences set to 'desire a particular type of car'.

This is In-perception® in action. The car becomes the object of a desire 'pattern match' whereby the human already desires such a car, either consciously or not, and when the car is observed, the In-perception® process automatically kicks in.

So, in this case, the In-perception® process described above would go something like this:

I see a car → I project desire onto the car → the car appears to project appeal back to me (but it's actually an echo of my thoughts) → my desire grows but I think, 'How can I afford such a car?' and I project that thought onto the car → the car might now become an object of frustration (because I assume I can't afford it) or an object of wanton desire (because I have money available and I can buy it) → so now I have a choice of letting my frustration getting the better of me and walking away annoyed with myself for not being as successful as I wanted to be, or I can plan how and when to buy the car, or I can just walk away realizing that the whole episode was made up by me in the first place!

The car knows nothing about this.

Imagine the In-perception® process with another human, both people projecting overlaying thoughts and feelings, creating false illusions onto each other.

Once we see this process, we can drop it and refresh our perception, falling out of the thought/feeling cycle and rebooting our personal version, and refreshing it with what is really out there:

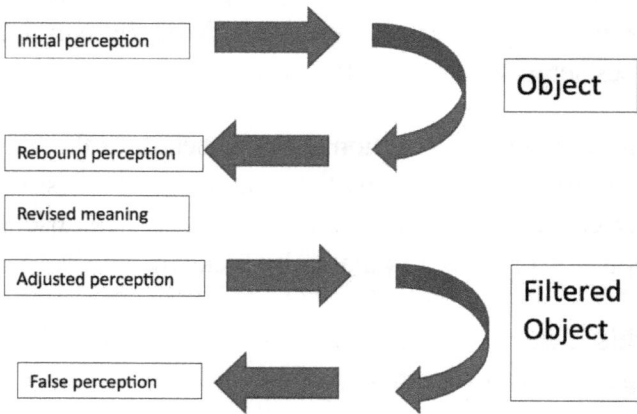

**Figure 9** In-perception®

This process operates one hundred per cent of the time, so think about how it also happens with other everyday objects such as spiders, heights, and clowns (producing phobias) and other human beings (producing lust and relationship issues).

Be careful not to be tricked by the echo of your own thoughts projected onto an innocent object.

In summary, In-perception® is the process that cycles or loops back layers of meaning, which appears to fabricate external reality with the power to influence behaviour or create feelings, and as the result of this illusory process, we can be persuaded to adapt to our environment when in fact the environment is neutral.

## How Thoughts Work with Our Perception of Time

Thoughts are not real in the sense of being part of the external material reality.

Like dreams, they are preform, operating inside the imagination in pictures, visions, ideas, suggestions in our internal commentary.

Memories are like phantom visions, present-time representations of an event that no longer exists other than in our imagination.

The mind recreates an event that is encoded as being in the 'past' but it can never be 'real' again, or even recalled exactly as it originally happened, because the mind does not record external events. Instead it uses In-perception® to project our mind-made perceptions so that they appear to be outside.

For example, if I had been surprised by the sudden appearance of a large spider when I was six years old, my mind logs that experience in my brain/body, encoding it as that experience, producing an inherent heightened awareness when it comes to spiders.

However, if I'm use it when I'm fifty years older, it becomes a faulty perception, because the system still uses it as a template unless I update it.

Effectively the old event is 're-remembered' and therefore re-encoded in the present time but referenced back to the original event in the brain's representation of time.

I am living in this moment, but my In-perception® of spiders is referencing an experience that happened when I was six years old.

This referencing is called the 'affect bridge' and gives us the illusory impression that we can bring feelings from the past, but because feelings are the principle of thought in action, we can only experience them in the present moment.

Feelings are not a principle in themselves, but they are the effect of the principle of thought, like a shadow.

A memory is an internal event, producing thought in the moment and the event cycle begins.

## Personal Time

We need to have 'time' as a function of our inner world to make sense of reality otherwise all our experiences would seem to be happening all at the same time!

The brain calibrates our experiences into a timeline that is unique to each of us. We can share experiences with others and agree that something happened at a certain time and place, such as the Twin Towers event in 9/11, but we often doubt our own memories.

Future visions are also not real but projections created by us using the principle of thought, but it is unlikely they will ever happen in the way we imagine them.

Having said that, there seems to be some evidence that if we imagine something vividly enough it may eventually take form, such as an illness or virus.

## Three Aspects of Thought?

Just like gravity, 'thought' is always happening, whether we want it to or not, but my experience is that thought can show up in different ways. So I've attempted to identify these three aspects of the same creative power:

**Pre-thought (or data-thought).** This is like 'live' creative energy flowing in preform from the source (we are all aware of the energy emanating from the same source which is sometimes called mind, universe, or God), creating reality around us and through us moment by moment. Pre-thought includes all quantum potential and is limitless, available for selective perception by every form of created entity, i.e. human, animal, insect, etc. and potentially includes every universe or multiverse as it is timeless and infinite. Some say that every creature experiences a version of reality upholstered or rendered specifically for them to gain maximum experience. A prime example of this is the way specific insects are attracted to specific plants so they can pollenate them.

**In-thought (or experiential thought).** This is moment-by-moment experience of live, real-time thought arising from our immediate experience. We experience in-thought as form or material reality and create an individual meaning in response to it, creating an interactive experience that loops back and forth creating a self-perpetuating loop, continuously updating via In-perception®. Each in-thought experience will vary depending on the creature's frame of reference or sensory receptors, e.g., human, animal, insect, etc. In-perception® describes the process that cycles or loops back layers of meaning, which appears to fabricate external reality with the power to influence behaviour or create feelings, and as a result of this illusory process, we can be persuaded to adapt to our environment, when in fact the environment is neutral.

**Phantom-thought** is the habitual, offline internal referencing system that appears to be coming from the past but is experienced in real time (these thoughts form the basis of our preferences or comfort zone and act like a cat's whisker in letting us know if it's ok to proceed beyond what we know). The 'cat's whisker' is a process that keeps us safe, but it can also keep us restricted and stuck. (I call this cat's whisker because it works in a way like the referencing system cats use to know whether it is safe to proceed into an unknown place, such as a gap in a fence or tight passageway. If the whiskers can fit, then the body will fit, avoiding the possibility of getting stuck and being unable to turn around and escape. The human referencing system will effectively check an external stimulus against our internal hard drive of previous experiences and be alerted by previous dangers experienced, consequently releasing appropriate chemicals into the body to motivate moving forward or retreating—anticipation or revulsion).

Our individual memories create an unreal experience of past-formed thoughts probably no longer relevant to our moment-to-moment experience, but all the same creating echo-feelings and emotions, which can trick us into thinking they are being created in the moment.

Maybe this is more prevalent in human experience as a system to protect, learn, and advance the species but due to the misunderstanding that our feelings are created from the outside-in, this gift is often misinterpreted as a problem rather than a guidance system. We experience past events from now, which is a different perspective and from a place that didn't exist when we had the original experience.

## Choices About Thoughts and Thinking

We experience internally the mystery of thought passing through our awareness or consciousness; therefore, we can choose to ignore individual thoughts, let them go or we can grab them, use them as a source of inspiration and turn them to action/behaviours.

That internal decision to let it go or not will have NO effect on external reality or other people until it manifests into behaviour.

We 'own' thoughts. They obey us, not the other way round. We should not be slaves to our thoughts.

Like leaves on a river, we can notice thoughts but let them float by.

Thoughts produced in the unrenewed mind are often:

- Tricky
- Seductive
- Suggestive
- Self-justifying
- Untrustworthy
- Uncontrolled
- Untamed
- Negative
- Earthly
- Downward

Remember, thoughts generate feelings.

Being upset by our thoughts is like writing ourselves a nasty letter and then being annoyed by it.

If our aim is to enjoy life, not to overthink it, then we can achieve this by creating some space between thoughts/feelings and 'self' such as using the Drop it! strategy (see later) or practising being in the space between or before thoughts begins (also see later).

## Analysis Paralysis

Contrary to popular belief, we have a choice to practice quietening down the analytical mind or to let it babble away, analysing, judging, and criticising, but each will produce different feelings.

The mind shows its creativity and intelligence in the way that it produces an endless stream of thoughts.

Pay attention to one and it can tag us along for a ride.

If we turn our attention to something else the thought often disappears, which shows how fleeting an event it really was.

Distraction is a great strategy for letting thoughts pass by.

Thoughts feed and grow in relation to the attention we give them.

When we get into intensive thinking or when a thought holds us, let it go because generally it will take us into memory.

Enjoy the quiet space.

Observe the quiet space.

Our core of wellbeing is healthy functioning.

In that space we can find space and peace. This is different from the intellectual aspect of the mind.

This is the nature of the mind's creative space and what arises in that space is:

- Not learnt
- Not in your core personality
- Not 'ego'

- Not personal-mind created
- Wisdom
- Common sense
- Like the bridge of the ship
- Centre
- Often obscured by 'learnt' thought processes and habitual thinking
- Like the child inside
- Intuitive
- Creative
- Inner peace
- Better and more powerful than the thought-machine
- Only operates in the present moment.

Our mind is often innocently responding according to our misunderstanding of how In-perception® works and often misses the point of the inside-out revelation.

This huge misunderstanding that our wellbeing comes from our circumstances or something outside of us, results in our mind being habitually programmed. When we are dissatisfied with life, the system automatically problem-solves for us but it automatically does it by prompting us to look externally for the cause, for external solutions such as a change of location, job, partner etc.

It's as if the habitual mind has a totally different agenda to the renewed mind. Which works from an inside-out setting.

The habitual me-first mind will feed us with such different suggestions from the renewed mind.

### The Unrenewed Mind (UM), or 'Personas', Versus the Renewed Mind (RM)

Here are some examples of the habitual preferences of the unrenewed mind and the renewed mind:

UM compares but RM views events without comparison.
UM contrasts and judges but RM creates connections.
UM uses analysis but the RM is creative.
UM is all about 'doing' but the RM is unconditional.
UM is task-oriented but RM is not situation-centred.
UM gets frustrated but RM has all the time it needs.
UM gets unhappy but RM is non-judgemental.
UM is striving but RM is content.
UM is by default negative but RM only sees now.
UM is conditional but RM is the observer of thoughts.
UM is life-situation centred but RM is a higher mind.
UM is time limited but RM is constant.
UM is self-judgemental but RM is just realistic and honest.
UM uses memory as a reference but RM is fresh and creative.
UM uses projection to create illusion but RM is creator of thought.
UM is insecure but RM is peace and connection to the Holy Spirit.

When we are aware of the In-perception® process, we have more choice as to the actions we can take.

Dwelling on thoughts gives them more energy, makes them grow, then that leads to another thought latching on until the 'train' is in full motion, a train of thought, moving like a runaway, and each thought casting a shadow of feeling, an emotion manifesting from it.

## Wisdom

Wisdom helps us sift the thoughts that are worth following or keeping.
Wisdom is not manipulated by thoughts.
Wisdom is more powerful, is more trustworthy.

Wisdom lies beyond thought, it can be heard in the space between the thoughts.
Wisdom will give solutions without thinking.

It will reassure you, asking where was the problem you had when you weren't thinking about it? It will be in the same place when I think about it or when I stop thinking about it.

Wisdom can have a sense of humour.

Let wisdom be your guide.

The ancestor of every action is a thought.

Remember the process: Thought (preform) → emotion (chemical urging) → action.

## The Pleasure Principle

The pleasure principle works on the basis that if we get instant gratification from an action, we are more likely to take that action than delay gratification for a longer-term gain.

An example of this is instant cream bun gratification versus long-term weight loss goals. This also involves a process called 'temporal discounting' where the brain weighs up the instant gain against the value of the long-term goal and decides for us that the instant gain is more fun!

It's impossible to feel gratitude for something when you are too busy trying to improve it.

The past was real once. Now it only exists in your imagination as a thought (echo-thought).

## Are We Who We Think We Are?

In-perception® warns us of the dangers of believing what we see to be absolutely true. It enables us to challenge our perception to test if it is real or influenced by thoughts from our past.

It enables us to question our thought systems, our thought filters, our preferences, and comfort zone understandings and check for any unconscious bias that might be influencing our psychological and spiritual freedom.

Try thinking from an alternative cultural perspective or as another person you know.

Use In-perception® to project different cultural values onto an object. For example, what is a ten-pound note when you have no awareness to project onto it?

As a child we learn to think/react as we were taught to. However, when we are grown up, with more wisdom and understanding (and hopefully more compassion), we should look to unlearn childish thinking habits and try different angles.

If you are thinking about a situation or event that occurred when you were a lot younger, then you are viewing that event now from a perspective that you never even considered could exist when you were younger.

For example, if you believe that you made a mistake or a misjudgement when you were sixteen and now you are fifty-six, it's as if you are a visitor from the future looking back on something that happened forty years ago.

Life was different, the environment was different, rules, society, and everything was so different.

We always make the best decision we can at the time with the information we have available to us at the time. How many people set out to make bad or stupid decisions, especially if they are living with the consequences of that decision forty years later and haven't done something about it!

So, our review of a past decision can be pointless unless we want to clear that template from the system as no longer appropriate or useful.

Choose wisdom, fresh from the now, from beyond your memory.

### Fresh Donuts are Available Every Day

The past has gone, and we have done what we have done. Forgive and move on.

Another example could be feeling defensive, or justifying actions, resulting from parental programming or a workplace mentality. This can be let go or rebooted by reviewing that old situation from the viewpoint of what you know now—as a wiser and more mature person.

Why would you want to carry around a bag full of echoes from the past?

### Does Cause and Effect Influence Our Thinking?

Thinking in terms of cause and effect leads to accepting conditioned responses to what appear to be external stimuli but are in fact projected echoes from ourselves.

There, projections are informed by our preferences. Consider this: Other cultures don't think this way, so we don't need to either.

Some psychologies might suggest that we are so heavily conditioned by past influences, which create a sort of script or schema for our future behaviour that it's difficult to change.

This is sometimes known as 'imprinting'. Imprinting suggests something permanent, but memory is only brought alive by thought in the moment, and thought is spiritual and doesn't take form until we give it permission to do so by using the principle of consciousness.

Belief in imprinting is a self-fulfilling prophecy—what we believe, we conceive, and we can really tell ourselves some great stories!

These stories, well, they validate themselves. We can become societally hypnotized into believing that critical parents beget critical kids, kind parents beget kind kids etc. (generally).

The total of all these conclusions is attitude. Attitude = thoughts believed to be true.

We can only begin to appreciate who we truly are when we lessen our need to prove ourselves to those who we assume have set the preferences for us in the first place.

If your parents insisted on perfection then to please them, you may, as a child, have repressed certain behaviours that proved you were not perfect, otherwise you might have not been acceptable to those perfect parents.

That is a self-imposed prison.

People are nearly always unaware of any such suggestion until a counsellor or therapist suggests it may be true and then, hey presto, there is a problem to solve which we might never have been aware of.

This might be useful in clearing an ingrained thought pattern, but equally it might create more issues and send us into deep analysis of our past. This is a risk with the something-wrong psychology.

The past is the past—forget it, move into reality.

Our parents did their best with the resources and knowledge they had and in the times in which they lived.

If you are told that you were not wanted as a child, then you can forget it now because you are not that child anymore. You give energy to that thought by believing it to still be true.

Whether your parents knew it or not, you were always going to turn up in some form or another and now that you have, you might as well make the most of the gift of life.

As we let go of thoughts of who we think we are (self-image, preferences) our insecurity begins to lift. It is then that we can begin to live outside our thought system (or ego).

It is then that we connect with our core selves and let the spirit renew our minds.

## In-perception® as Our Conscious Filter

If I mention the term 'ego', it means the 'self' as envisaged by us—the projected self-image which believes that it lives at the centre of the universe, according to the old mind.

The ego could also have been called 'me' or 'self' or 'personal mind', and it is a reasonable assumption that all your misconceptions and mistaken beliefs stick to this ego.

The ego seriously influences what we project onto the world around us.

The ego uses In-perception® to manipulate and even bully other people. It creates false templates and holds in place such disorders as borderline personality disorder leading to false accusations based on our misinformed projections, believing them to be real.

Ego of the Devil is what infected Eden and has grown like a virus infecting every innocent human being throughout time until that moment when God whispers into our soul that he's calling us home.

So, as we realise that the ego is a self-fulfilling prophetic construct and that we are much more than that, insecure thinking patterns drop away. We begin to experience natural feelings of self-esteem, gratitude for what we are, not what we do.

We are human beings, not human doings.

We are not defined by what we do, own, or have but rather that we exist, have consciousness, and a free will to do with that what we will.

Without the pressure of having to maintain our ego (personas to impress other people) or thought-created persona (who we think we are), we relax, and enjoy whatever we are doing at a moment.

Dropping ego lets us see new options, alternatives.

We are no longer acting along preprogrammed assumptions and preferences that we are a particular type of person or a collection of persons depending on whom it is we are trying to impress, so that we can keep our relationship or our job or our material possessions.

We are free.

In-perception® breaks the illusion of a reality created by our ego, that illusion that what we see is the only reality that exists for us.

Now, realise that all the other innocent sufferers of insecurity, isolation, lostness, and fear are unaware, trapped in the old legacy mind of fear, limitation, and insecurity.

None of us are responsible until we realise that we are, and then we have the choice.

That's why and when our compassion grows, and we have shifted into a higher level of conscious awareness we begin to realise what life is really all about.

## Choice Points

As we come to this point of choice, as we enter a new level of conscious awareness, choices appear:

Acting from life or death?
Acting from love or thinking?
Acting from truth or analysis?
Acting from love or anger?
Acting from forgiveness or grudges?
Letting go or dwelling on it?
Not having to be right or being right?
Letting go or hanging on?
Light thinking or complicated thinking?
Little or no analysis or thorough analysis?
It's ok or it's NOT ok?
I don't need to go there, or I need to go there?

## Do We Create Our Negative Mindsets?

Some research suggests that ninety per cent of our old-mind thinking is negative, allegedly.

Be selective, choose what to think about, choose to love instead of to fear.

Be careful about what you read. Like other people's personal-mind, fictional creations, or other people's 'how to' insights and wisdom, that was ok at a particular moment in time, for them, but is completely inappropriate for you now because you are in a different time and context—think about that!

Be careful what you watch on TV (news is generally about what might have happened and what might happen in the future so it's not real), talk radio (opinions of others), because we mimic this stuff.

Life experience is related to where we choose to focus our attention.

Don't play out the scenarios in your mind unless you aware of what you are doing.

In NLP there is a technique whereby, if you are in a quandary as to what direction to choose or road to pursue, you are encouraged to 'run the movie' and notice your feelings and the responses of other people when you imagine that you have followed each option.

The imagination is great for this—it's like a reality generator and, because the brain/body doesn't know the difference between a real event and a vividly imagined event, you will get a reaction from the body as to which is the preferred or more comfortable path to choose.

So use the wisdom that In-perception® gives you to run movies to see what your mind is projecting and what you are believing is real, then run a different movie and see what happens.

Of course, this is just an option. What is more fun is to just show up and follow your wisdom and see what unfolds moment to moment.

## More Choice

Other options when confronted by choice are:

Do nothing.
Wait.
Let the moment arise and pass.

Avoid pre-empting or preprograming your brain to anticipate the next scenario or you will see what you expect to see rather than the pure potential that's there for you.

Avoid creating imaginary problems that may never come into being.

This is one of the problems with doing the run the movie exercise because the brain can begin to reference past experiences and insert them into future events. That will maybe put you off taking a particular course of action which in real time might be an exciting option.

All this reflection and rumination on the past causes you harm and creates anticipatory chemical injection to influence behaviour.

Remember thinking works in pictures, movies, and internal dialogue.

Avoid allowing the internal dialogue to run everyday life.

## Future Scenarios

The first thing that gets generated into a future scenario is the 'I' self-image (ego), not the core.

What I mean by that is that we think of a future situation, and we create a version of the self to project into that future, but that projection is not wholly us—it is a self-created, partial construct, imperfect in the whole, and that construct becomes the internal template that we then must pattern match to when the actual event comes.

For example, if we must make a public presentation, we might use a technique to create a projected self-image that is confident and relaxed and calm and so we run that in our imagination, and it all seems ok. But then when the real event occurs, we must pattern match to that template otherwise it feels uncomfortable. Trouble is, that is not really us!

The real event, when it arrives, will never be the same as we have imagined it!

## Overcoming Fear of Future

A different approach might be to just show up for the presentation and allow wisdom to guide us as to how we should be and what we should say.

Fear of our experience is a killer of inspiration and 'flow'.

Negative thoughts = negative feelings.

Negative thought leads to In-perception® projection of the 'I' that isn't real or the best version of you to deal with the situation that is about to occur.

The accumulation factor applies here.

What I mean by that is that fundamentally each of us is unique, like multifaceted diamonds—beautiful, and we reflect the environment we find ourselves in, moment to moment.

Trouble is, to please others and be acceptable during our growing years (when the brain isn't fully formed), we don't have the critical faculty to question others and so accept what they say to keep the peace.

It's like we are covering that diamond with layer upon layer of manure, but then we've also covered the manure with varnish to impress others.

Those layers of manure need elimination.

However, to do that we have to break through the varnish that we have applied as a way of covering up and putting on a show to the world.

To break those old habits takes courage.

Fear sits within the preferences relevant to the projected 'I', so if you change the projected 'I', fear may not accompany it.

Use the In-perception® model to identify where ego is projecting past characteristics onto your present experience and see if you can change that.

If there's a void, fill it with wisdom, inspired stuff. Deep stuff, good, beautiful stuff.

Watch the river flow.

We become what we think about all day long. Live in the moment.

Release ties to the past and stop speculating about the future.

Dismiss random thoughts; bring attention back to what you are doing.

To paraphrase mindfulness teacher John Kabat-Zinn, wherever you go, you will always be there.

No need to hurry, because life isn't an emergency, it's an experience.

Take rewards now, not in the future. The pleasure principle is there to make life acceptable, enjoyable, and the fun ride it should be.

Present-moment thinking allows you to forgive anyone and everyone, which in turn frees you once and for all to enjoy your life, as you deserve to.

'Life is what's happening while you're making other plans.' John Lennon.

## Healthy Functioning Versus Unhealthy Analytical Thinking

We have a choice to either live from moment to moment or to live influenced by our past and worried about our future. The words on the left might describe our always present (innate) mental wellbeing but which often lay beneath the veil of contaminated, habitual, superstitious thinking (the words on the right side of the list).

| Healthy thinking from innate wellbeing | Unhealthy thinking from habitual patterns |
|---|---|
| Mind clear and free | Mind full of worry and concerns |
| Seeing innocence | Seeing evil and conspiracy |
| Focus on beautiful | Focus on ugliness |
| Happy with what is (content) | Obsessed with betterment |
| Experiencing life | Analysing life |
| Letting go | Hanging on |
| Flowing thinking | Computer thinking |
| Focus on what you can change | Focus on what you can't change |
| Learning from mistakes and moving on | Dwelling and repeating |
| Open and accepting | Closed and prejudiced |
| Positive attitude | Negative attitude |

The veil is not natural, it is learnt from conditioning, parents, school, culture, etc. and is maintained by the need for acceptance, security, and fear. It is the system, and we maintain it ourselves through our 'I' preferences.

How to get around the analytical mind? Drop the thought and clear your head.

**Choice Point?**

Swing the pendulum from right to left.

Feelings are the guide for now until we learn how faith works.

We already know what to do. It's only conditioning and fear that stops us.

If we hadn't learnt to feel defensive, we would not feel it.

Don't keep score—let it go.

The greatest breakthrough is letting go of the need to be right.

'There is no right or wrong, only thinking makes it so.' William Shakespeare.

Mental problems and unhappiness are the result of becoming over-absorbed by our own negative thinking while at the same time being unaware that we are the one who is thinking.

## Mapping Our World

When anything is forgotten or dismissed, it doesn't mean that it doesn't exist in your experience, because it's going to be logged in the memory.

You will not be affected by anything that doesn't exist in your reality (on your map*), but memories infect and influence our map and will be triggered by real-time events.

By the term 'map', I am referring to the metaphorical example that we create an internal map of the world to make sense of it. Every individual's map is different because of our preferences. The map is not the territory, just as the map of the London Tube system isn't the tube system but represents it in a way that provides sufficient information to get around and travel from A to B.

Similarly, we could never hold all of 'reality' in our heads, so we create a map that is sufficient to get us about.

The secret of an amazing life is to constantly update and enrich that map otherwise we just get stuck and believe that what we have on our map is all there is.

## The Psychological Principles of Life

A principle is something that is applicable regardless of the specifics of any given situation.

Details, however, are variables that differ from one situation to the next.

As a thought stays with us, as we focus on it, it begins to have an effect on the way we feel. Even a thought about a minor issue such as a person driving slowly in front of us can motivate us to crazy actions if it doesn't leave our mind quickly enough.

We have the ability, should we choose it, to make any thoughts as permanent as we wish. This is precisely why so many people live in an almost constant state of frustration and irritation often over trivial things.

It's impossible to feel jealous without first having jealous thoughts. It's the same with anger, worry, fear, guilt, etc.

How do those labelled thoughts present themselves to you? How can you recognise them and the shadow feelings that accompany them?

## Can You Let Your Thoughts Pass?

Can you recognise thoughts that are self-perpetuated and materialise in the form of images, internal dialogue, or both?

These are false images, preform, with no effect on the external material world.

There is no such thing as real feelings either because they are all phantoms, arising from internally created thoughts.

It might appear that they are arising from what is happening outside, but they are arising from internally created thoughts about the external stimulus.

Therefore, we create the way we feel one hundred per cent of the time.

So, use the mind as a tool. Dismiss random thoughts and use the mind to 'think as directed by you' or, in other words, 'think on purpose'.

## Wisdom is From Beyond the Personal Mind

Wisdom is not tied to intelligence or intellect—it comes from a different place—it exists beyond our personal ego in the creative, impersonal part of mind that is flowing through us.

Principles practitioners generally attribute wisdom to the intelligence of universal mind and, if we have chosen to live in accordance with biblical principles, then of course wisdom is from God's Holy Spirit and it will bring to the new mind wisdom from the creator of life itself.

Recognising and tuning into wisdom is like going 'online' and tapping into the creative energy that is writing the experience of life moment to moment.

The personal mind is like a disc that's running on the hard drive of the brain, but wisdom is like live streaming, in-game instructions and guidance.

There is nothing to be frightened of regarding your own thoughts or feelings—there is nothing they can do to hurt you.

'If the one thing people learnt was not to be afraid of their experience it would change the world.' Sydney Banks.

Don't fight the mind. That's a civil war.

Rather than fighting your thoughts, wishing them away or pushing them away, you can begin to feel empowered by the knowledge that you are the one who is thinking them. Trust you can help yourself by letting them drift from your consciousness.

'The solution to a problem will never come about from the same level of understanding that created the problem in the first place.' Albert Einstein.

Don't anticipate but participate. Then let it go.

Each individual person has a curriculum (preferences, agenda) and every curriculum can be overcome and conquered.

Every curriculum has a solution.

When the game changes, that can be the moment when we realise that there is something other than ourselves spinning this planet and ensuring the seasons happen on time.

## Innate Wellbeing

Nourish that part of yourself that you now know exists and is healthy—your innate wellbeing.

While every curriculum is unique, every solution is identical by realising the power of thought.

Most of us forget that we are the one doing the thinking and that we are actively manufacturing the thoughts we think.

Our innate wellbeing will always arise when we drop out of unhelpful thinking.

## Shifting Through the Thinking Gears

Shift from negative to positive in these three steps:

Recognise and admit the habit of thinking. Understand that thoughts originate with me and I create my own experience of life. See the innocence of negative thinking.

The way you look at life isn't something that happens to you—it's something you make up moment by moment as you move through life.

At any moment in your life, you can decide to change your attitude.

Your attitude is made up of one thing and one thing only—your own thoughts.

Change them and your world will change in an instant.

You feel the way you do because of the thoughts you are having.

The lack of happiness, the uneasy feeling, the dysfunction, comes from the fact that your thoughts do not align with wisdom, which shows up in your feelings.

You think one thing and feel another, and this misalignment causes internal conflict.

Other people give you advice and you feel obliged to comply but internally your own wisdom is disputing the advice. You feel that you can't say no because you risk rejection but it's all just thinking.

Here's the conundrum; We use In-perception® to project our thoughts onto the external world, which we consequently observe as having those qualities that we ourselves projected onto it.

## Happiness

There is no one way to happiness. Happiness *is* the way.

Happiness is an innate quality of the human system, a feeling you tap into, not an outcome of external events that you can't control.

Feelings are your happy meter.

The act of admitting that you are creating feelings of depression for yourself through your own thinking is a very empowering and healing admission.

## Gratitude

Gratitude is natural—you have to learn not to be grateful. Notice when gratitude is there. Attend to the feeling. Make it grow.

There is something you can do to create your experience of life. You don't need to produce thoughts and then be depressed by those thoughts. Thoughts come and go like a river carrying leaves. Your mind produces a never-ending supply of thoughts. Some are nice, some are not.

They are just thoughts.

You reach.

You grab hold.

It's *your* choice.

Your attention is the only glue holding your thinking in place.

Live in the present moment.

Keep a check on where your thoughts are focused—past, present, or future?

Drop past and future, they are just echoes.

Attend to now.

Live your life in the present moment and be grateful that you have this moment.

# Chapter Six

# Paradigm Shift: Psycho–Spiritual Psychology

## Introduction

*So far we have explored the mind's operating principles, how we process events (event cycle), how we can break habitual patterns (conscious levels) and how we project our own reality onto others (In-perception®).*

*So now I turn to more explanation about the origin of the discovery of the principles and how this discovery is unifying the field of psychology, not only from the many and fractured theories of the past, but by also healing the rift between the material and spiritual parts of the human nature.*

*In 1973, Sydney Banks, a Scottish welder of basic education, had an enlightenment experience which led to a burgeoning community of psychologists and therapists coming together across the world over the intervening years, testing and honing his revelation about psychological principles and distilling them down to the Three Principles. At the time, Syd believed that he'd seen 'God' and what he'd received would change psychiatry and psychology forever. The Church rejected it, universities rejected it, psychology sort of accepted it conditionally, but now, fifty years later its efficacy is proven. If this is true, then it is a paradigm shift in our understanding of how the mind works. This chapter is a short summary article which I wrote in 2013 in an effort to explain to my clients what I was trying to guide them to see for themselves.*

## What is a Paradigm Shift?

In science and technology, a new revelation about how something works makes any previous theory obsolete.

For example, when it was uncovered that the earth was a globe rather than flat, falling off the edge became a ludicrous idea, an obsolete theory.

Facts always trump theories.

Facts and a paradigm shift always wake us up to what's next.

## A Paradigm Shift in Mental Health and Wellbeing

For many years I've been providing therapy, education, and training, which is grounded in the Three Principles, which is a natural, non-theoretical understanding of human functioning that applies to everyone.

I've found that an understanding of this functioning virtually eliminates anxiety, revealing deeper levels of mental health, emotional resilience, and creative thinking leading to inner peace and better relationships with others.

How does this work?

To allow this natural understanding to flourish, we must first correct innocent but life-changing misunderstandings about human functioning that have been the cause of anxiety, fear, insecurity, and feeling lost in life for so many people.

These misunderstandings are about the true nature of our thinking, our feelings, and our identity.

We will automatically get free from unnecessary psychological suffering by correcting these innocent misunderstandings that have become engrained in our cultural beliefs about psychology and spirituality.

When working with clients for change, these are the two primary misunderstandings that we explore and that will potentially create a strong foundation for change:

## Misunderstanding #1

Thoughts and feelings are two separate things.

No, they are two aspects of the same psychological function, and it is only innocently well-meaning theories from the past that have separated them.

## Misunderstanding #2

Human beings are just physical beings.

No, Human beings are more than physical and are always functioning simultaneously both physically and spiritually and, again, it is only innocently well-meaning theories from the past that have separated them.

Why is this relevant to helping people today?

## Thoughts and Feelings

When thoughts and feelings are separated, we must find a source for our feelings and so we look around for causes and innocently become victims of a world 'out there'. We naturally assume that if we want to change our feelings, we need to change something about the world. When we reunite thought and feelings as inseparable aspects of our psychological functioning, and we come to understand that feelings are part of an internally generated experience, we can stop mistakenly attributing feelings to our circumstances or other people. This corrects the need for huge amounts of unnecessary thinking, worry, and anxiety and the mistaken need to make changes outside to change feelings inside. It all becomes an inside job.

## Physical and Spiritual

When theories suggested separation of the two aspects of the human being this caused an illusion of duality between the physical and the spiritual, which has ultimately led us to underlying feelings of insecurity and loss of identity. In this fractured state, separated by a misdirection that the Church would deal with spirit and psychologists would deal with the psyche, we have lost our true selves and even more practically, we've lost awareness of the true nature of thought, which is the link between the two states. In addition, spirituality has become something we have to strive for and achieve rather than something we already have. This again creates an illusion that some people are more 'spiritual' than others.

When understanding reunites our physical and spiritual aspects we come home to ourselves, effectively meeting our 'other half' and we no longer need to search outside for that either.

This too becomes an inside job.

## Simplifying the Process of Mental and Emotional Healing

Once we see that we have innocently created the reason for our own distress we can focus on what is important, rather than what is no longer required. That's a load of worry off our minds.

As we innocently created fractured beliefs about human functioning, we began to call it the 'human condition' and that mysterious term that apparently many of us suffer from, seemed to be good enough, but I was never satisfied with it. If so, then it should now just be a case of replacing those incorrect beliefs with common sense facts. That's not been as easy as it might seem.

Not everybody is willing to give up well-established beliefs and patterns of thinking.

## Paradigm Shift

In science and business, major changes in understanding are called paradigm shifts.

A paradigm can be defined as a way of thinking about something, usually by most people.

The problem with paradigm shifts is that, at first, not everybody goes along with the changes.

Examples of paradigm shifts that didn't catch on at first are many. The medical world didn't accept germ theory at first, staying with beliefs that diseases were caused by bad smells. The scientific world denied Galileo's sun-centric model of the solar system and there is still a flat earth society despite thousands of satellites orbiting the globe.

Paradigm shifts always reveal what has always been the case rather than creating something new, but it often has the appearance of something new.

So I operate based on a paradigm shift in the field of psychology, which makes an adjustment and corrects something that was actually never true in the first place.

## A Bit of History

Around a hundred years ago, an American psychologist William James said that if psychological principles were ever discovered it would unify the field and turn psychology into a science and a philosophy. It seems that the unifying principles have now been uncovered and have been brought into the public domain through a most unlikely source that seems to have bypassed the gatekeepers of the pre-paradigm forms of the profession in both the psychological and spiritual worlds.

When Sydney Banks had his spontaneous spiritual enlightenment experience it was revealed to him the oneness of all things and from this experience he started to help others, through a field of psychology that he came to call the Three Principles: these are universal mind, consciousness and thought.

Universal mind is the name Syd gave to the intelligent energy or life force behind all things. Universal thought is the name Syd gave to the creative energy of that life force that humans can use, and universal consciousness is the name he gave to our ability to be aware of this process happening moment by moment, not just via the senses but in a deeper way, throughout our body, as feelings.

Understanding that these are universal principles (universal means they're common to everyone irrespective of age, culture, status, and education) is the first step to any meaningful life change, because this creates a paradigm shift in our understanding. The result of that is that we no longer need to focus on behaviour to make changes, but we focus on what is creating the behaviour.

Under the old mistaken understanding, we might have a pattern formula something like this:

Thought + feelings = motivation = behaviour/action.

Once we reunite thought and feelings and realise the nature of thought, we have broken the pattern, corrected the misunderstanding and rebooted our understanding of what we experience every moment of every day.

Thought/feelings = experience.

This breaks habits, releases us to live each experience without fear and ends the confusion of theoretical concepts about the human condition, which are the root causes of mental instability, overthinking, and anxiety.

We are free to act or not, depending on information available to us at any given moment, no longer based on experience, habitual patterns of thought, and fears about the future.

We are free to function in the moment and that, I promise you, takes a load off my mind and it will take a load off yours too.

Working from a principles-based understanding of the human function we drop non-factual theories that were based on best information available at the time they were conceived. We look at everything from the simple basis of mind, consciousness, and thought and that takes us automatically in the direction of what is creating our moment-to-moment experience rather than what has already been created. When we see that we are the co-creators of our experience, we can work with the implications of that.

# Chapter Seven

# Spiritual Reunification

## Introduction

*This is a bridge section between the more psychological focus of Part One and the spiritual and supernatural aspects of being fully human covered in Parts Two and Three.*

*I start with my own backstory of working in psychotherapy and how I discovered that we need to acknowledge the spiritual in our lives, otherwise we are effectively living life with one eye closed and one arm tied behind our backs.*

*Whether our spirituality is Bible-based or from another set of beliefs, spirit expands our experience beyond our everyday activities that tend to die when we do, metaphorically or realistically.*

## Divisions, Splits and Schisms

It is a natural part of the life cycle that cells divide, and this division creates new entities, but is this phenomenon always healthy and creative in the world that is already formed and operating?

One such example is when psychology divided from the Church and a humanistic, non-spiritual model of the human began to emerge.

From that division emerged two ways of being in the world, one based on spirit, the other on an autonomic flesh model where humans are random and short-lived.

If we were from the spiritual understanding, we kept going to some kind of church for our guidance and wellbeing. If we chose the psychological option, we went to psychiatrists and therapists and scientists instead.

I'm not saying that the split was perfect, there are many spiritual scientists and therapists just as there are atheists running churches, but in my experience of psychology and spirituality in most of the people I've worked with, both these aspects of our humanity are evident, although the trend now is therapy over prayer and CBT over natural healing.

My concern is why Bible-believing Christians would go for the humanistic psychological approach when Jesus clearly stated, 'For God is spirit, so those who worship him must worship in spirit and truth,' (John 4:24, NIV).

I think it will be useful here to quickly summarise the history of humanistic psychology from around the time that it split from the Church as an option for understanding and healing the human mind and the way something-wrong psychology has led us away from our innate natural health.

## A Short, Relevant History of Psychology

Psychology: study of the human mind and its functions, especially those affecting behaviour (source: an online dictionary).

I wasn't sure where to fit this into the narrative, so I've parked it here because it occurred to me that it was important to stress the dichotomy between God's plan for us and our own search for meaning.

Psychology of the soul, without the spirit of truth, is typical of the horizontal conscious level because we can only see what's obvious to the me-first personal mind.

As I explored how principles-based psychology could be more useful to people who believed in God but were still stressed, I thought it useful to summarise some of the pre-paradigm theories about the human condition that have been prominent in psychology over the past hundred and fifty years or so.

While psychology did not really emerge as a separate discipline until the late 1800s, its earliest history can be traced back to the early Greeks.

Psychology, as a field of experimental study, probably began in 1854 in Leipzig, Germany when Gustav Fechner created the first theory of how judgements about sensory experiences are made and how to experiment on them.

We can see how, even at this early developmental stage of psychology, the human propensity to question and look for meaning in the personal experience was being explored.

Fechner began delving more deeply into philosophy and conceived of a highly animistic (spiritual) universe with God as its soul. He discussed his idea of a universal consciousness at length in a work containing his plan of psychophysics. His health broke down several years later; his partial blindness and painful sensitivity to light likely developed because of his gazing at the sun during the study of visual afterimages. Madness is easily come by!

During the seventeenth century, the French philosopher Rene Descartes introduced the idea of dualism, which asserted that the mind and body were two entities that interact to form the human experience.

Many other issues still debated by psychologists today, such as the relative contributions of nature versus nurture, are rooted in these early philosophical traditions.

Also, during the mid-1800s, a German physiologist named Wilhelm Wundt was using scientific research methods to investigate reaction times. In his book published in 1873, *Principles of Physiological Psychology*, he outlined many of the major connections between the science of physiology and the study of human thought and behaviour.

Psychology flourished in America during the period of the mid- to late-1800s.

William James emerged as one of the major American psychologists during this period, publishing his classic textbook, *The Principles of Psychology*, which established him as the 'father of American psychology'. His book soon became the standard text in psychology and his ideas eventually served as the basis for a new school of thought known as functionalism. James said that if psychological principles were ever discovered it would unify the field and turn psychology into a science and a philosophy.

Up to this point, early psychology stressed conscious human experience.

An Austrian physician named Sigmund Freud changed the face of psychology in a dramatic way, proposing a theory of personality that emphasized the importance of the unconscious mind. Freud's clinical work with patients suffering from hysteria and other ailments led him to believe that early childhood experiences and unconscious impulses contributed to the development of adult personality and behaviour.

In his book, *The Psychopathology of Everyday Life*, Freud detailed how these unconscious thoughts and impulses are expressed, often through slips of the tongue (known as Freudian slips) and dreams. According to Freud, psychological disorders are the result of these unconscious conflicts becoming extreme or unbalanced.

The psychoanalytic theory proposed by Sigmund Freud has had a huge impact on twentieth-century thought, influencing the mental health field as well as other areas including art, literature, and popular culture. While many of his ideas are viewed with scepticism today, his influence on psychology is undeniable.

Carl Jung, a student of Freud's, has been a bit of a light in the darkness for God in the story of psychology. His spiritual views clashed with Freud's humanistic theories, and they split acrimoniously as Jung set out on his journey in a vastly different direction. Jungian psychology still holds many wonders for those searching the riches of God but also many of Jung's techniques have been adopted into the mainstream.

Psychology changed dramatically during the early twentieth century as another school of thought known as behaviourism rose to dominance. Behaviourism was a major change from previous theoretical perspectives, rejecting the emphasis on both the conscious and unconscious mind. Instead, behaviourism strove to make psychology a more scientific discipline by focusing purely on observable behaviour.

Behaviourism holds that the subject matter of human psychology is the behaviour of the human being. Behaviourism claims that consciousness is neither a definite nor a usable concept. The behaviourist, who has been trained always as an experimentalist, holds, further, that belief in the existence of consciousness goes back to the ancient days of superstition and magic.

The impact of behaviourism was enormous, and this school of thought continued to dominate for the next fifty years.

Psychologist B. F. Skinner furthered the behaviourist perspective with his concept of operant conditioning which demonstrated the effect of punishment and reinforcement on behaviour.

While behaviourism eventually lost its dominant grip on psychology, the basic principles of behavioural psychology are still widely in use today.

While the first half of the twentieth century was dominated by psychoanalysis and behaviourism, a new school of thought known as humanistic psychology emerged during the second half of the century. Often referred to as the 'third force' in psychology, this theoretical perspective emphasized conscious experiences. (This was the primary basis of my training as a psychotherapist, with a nod to Freud.)

American psychologist Carl Rogers is often considered to be one of the founders of this school of thought. While psychoanalysts looked at unconscious impulses and behaviourists focused on environmental causes, Rogers believed strongly in the power of free will and self-determination.

Psychologist Abraham Maslow also contributed to humanistic psychology with his famous hierarchy of needs theory of human motivation. This theory suggested that people were motivated by increasingly complex needs. Once the most basic needs are fulfilled, people then become motivated to pursue higher-level needs.

During the 1950s and 1960s, a movement known as the cognitive revolution began to take hold in psychology. During this time, cognitive psychology began to replace psychoanalysis and behaviourism as the dominant approach to the study of psychology. Psychologists were still interested in looking at observable behaviours, but they were also concerned with what was going on inside the mind.

Since that time, cognitive psychology has remained a dominant area of psychology as researchers continue to study things such as perception, memory, decision-making, problem-solving, intelligence, and language.

The introduction of brain imaging tools such as MRI and PET scans have helped improve the ability of researchers to more closely study the inner workings of the human brain.

Today, most psychologists do not identify themselves with a single school of thought, focusing instead on a particular speciality area or perspective, often drawing on ideas from a range of theoretical backgrounds. This eclectic approach has contributed new ideas and theories that would have continued to shape psychology for years to come if the Three Principles hadn't emerged as a major alternative fact-based understanding from the 1970s through to present time.

Human-centred psychology that puts 'self' first has led us away from dependence on God as our source and shifted us towards self-focus, drawing us to try to repair a mind that God long ago considered so useless that it was declared as good as dead.

If you are a Bible believer, please reflect again on Paul's letters to the Corinthian Church. He stressed the power of Christ in healing and maintaining a strong mind and warned against the humanistic wisdom of words that philosophers of the time used to keep people in confusion and elevate themselves above God.

## The Power of Principles in Psychology

Principles-based psychology is a new paradigm partly because it is not another theory or a therapeutic approach.

It is more concerned with the way the human operating system functions, and it is incorrect use of the system that creates psychological problems and maintains the illusion of separation from God.

A principle is a fact that is true irrespective of whether we personally believe it or not.

As previously mentioned, gravity is a principle. It's always on, always working and we cannot live without it as it is part of the structure that holds everything together and although it is invisible, we feel the effects of it all the time. Try letting go of a pen and see if it floats.

The principles of thought and consciousness are not self-centred, they are universal, common to all and so they can help us in our transition from the old me-first mind to the new other-first mindset.

As Paul pointed out in his letters, the renewed mind is the place where the human and Holy Spirits commune and decisions about behaviours and actions are decided. By using the principles of thought and consciousness we have tools that make those difficult internal conversations more manageable and communion with God's Holy Spirit more tangible.

I don't see these principles as another form of psychology or even a progression of theories because the principles have always been operating. They are not so much a discovery as an 'uncovery' of a pre-existing fact that all previous theories have innocently been built upon.

The principles illuminate how within the mind, consciousness and thought enable us as individuals to bring our passions and inspirations into reality whether that is the study and development of humans themselves or their lived environment through nature, building, social, and commercial development, and growth.

## Reunification

Ironically, it is by progressing to the adoption of a psychology that existed before all of the humanistic theories that we can reunite spirit and soul. We can correct the innocent misunderstanding that evolved through individual behaviourism that we are not lost souls, victims of an outside-in world, but limitless wellsprings of joy, peace, and wellbeing either in or outside of the Christian community.

Understanding the principles as *divine* mind, consciousness, and thought, we identify the spiritual tools that God has revealed. They enable us to see beyond our preconceived, outside-in, conditioned personal mind and see the 'patterns of this world' for what they truly are—deceptive, destructive, and based on a very clever deception about the existence and trustworthiness of God the creator.

God has revealed to the world of psychology that we have these psycho–spiritual gifts through which we have divine intelligence that will guide us and help us navigate life from moment to moment.

Syd Banks called the principles the missing link and I see them as our bridge between the visible dimension of earth and the invisible dimension of heaven.

We are all inclusive of God's purpose the earth. Even before we uncover God for ourselves and start to believe or are born again, we can realise our connection to the intelligence that spins the planet, organises the seasons, and provides the innate intelligence that all sentient creatures use to survive.

We have unlimited use of the divine mind that is vastly bigger and more powerful and more accessible than we have been led to believe.

Divine mind is not the human collective mind because it is heavenward rather that earthbound. Yes, we can find inspiration in so-called group-thought, but that is often still limited to horizontal-plane psychology. A member of the group might be more spiritual and influence the group, but there needs to be union in communion.

## The Outside-In Misunderstanding

We have all innocently set our minds to work according to the outside-in model which is founded on us being lost individuals searching for something 'out there' to complete us, separate from nature and competing for limited resources.

Pre-principles psychology, which is based on any of the theories from the past two hundred years, isn't working because it assumes an outside-in model, such as that if we change our circumstances, our partners, our job, our house then we will be happier when we know by experience that rarely is a sustainable solution. Or, if we understand our past, it will change our perception of the present and enable us to live a better future.

The outside-in misunderstanding enforces a something-wrong psychological model.

To access the divine with its power to renew our personal, habitual mind's outside-in conditioning, we need to go deeper than our personal intellectual understanding which is based on the misunderstanding, and allow a deeper consciousness to arise.

## Integrating Spiritual Nature with Psychology

I practised as an integrative psychotherapist using traditional outside-in techniques for five years or so before hearing about this new principles-based understanding that was producing powerful results in challenging communities such as prisons, education, and across the professional world of improving mental health.

Since that time, I have witnessed the growth of this principles-based model and, more recently, primarily through the relatively recent expansion in life coaching as a positive intervention, rather than traditional counselling or psychoanalysis.

The past ten years has seen a huge growth in people entering the personal coaching profession.

Due to increasing insecurity in the corporate world and a desire to be more in control of their destiny, people have left structured employment to start their own practices.

Rather than going through the four-year practice period required to become qualified as counsellors, people can gain a level of expertise (and insurance) to begin trading as a coach within months.

With very little regulation in coaching, people from various backgrounds have entered and transformed the self-help industry beyond recognition, giving clients more options to overcome their issues.

YouTube has enabled anyone to become a media star if they understand the algorithms that can get them to the top listings, plying their trade and appearing as experts in their chosen field, whether business coaching or personal transformation.

When experiencing personal freedom from their psychological issues, people are often motivated to start helping others, so they join the ever-growing number of full- or part-time coaches.

I had decided that my therapeutic life coaching career would be founded on a mental health baseline rather than business or self-development coaching.

I practised initially as a hypnotherapist. Hypnotherapy was very popular in the 1990s, particularly promoted by the likes of Paul Mckenna, through whom I discovered NLP. However, coaching is incredibly competitive so I needed a different angle, something that was unique and appealed to the more 'spiritual' inhabitants of the towns and villages where I worked.

It was during this time that the NLP teacher, Michael Neill, discovered Sydney Bank's work on the Principles and wrote about them in his ground-breaking book, "The Inside Out Revolution" through which many of my clients found freedom from their psychological problems.

I trained with one of his coaches, Jamie Smart, for two years, gaining certification in Jamie's branding of the Principles: a "Clarity" practitioner, coach, and trainer.

Without realising it, in training and practising in hypnotherapy and principles spirituality, I had forsaken my Christian roots and the personal care and love of God through Jesus who had changed my life so radically in 1988.

Instead of becoming more enlightened, I was becoming more troubled in my inner life through spiritual compromise, and my relationships and practice began to fail. I woke up to what had happened and tried to get back into the Christian life, but my unusually random personal situation and involvement with non-biblical spirituality was viewed with suspicion by many in traditional Church circles. It made it difficult to reconnect with a Church that would accept a twice-divorced man, carrying the questionable spiritual legacy of an understanding that had become popular in non-Christian circles.

In fairness, it wasn't surprising because in the early days of my initial Christian experience I myself had actually been warned to beware of spiritual practices that smelled of the occult. Clearly this had partially been the cause for me to fall away from my personal relationship with the God of the Bible.

It was in 2021 when my second marriage was ending that the miracle of God's love really broke through and just like in Jesus's parable of the Prodigal Son, my heavenly father welcomed me back into His fold, caring and soothing me through a difficult divorce and bowel cancer to a new relationship and marriage to a Christian woman who had been praying for years for a Christian husband.

After a year of proving to my old Church friends that I was trustworthy and re-establishing myself in an active community Church, I am being inspired to bring this logical psycho–spiritual aspect of the principles into the Church community as a viable and safe alternative to secular psychological approaches.

## Enlightenment in the Church?

I do not want to compromise, and I do not want to shy away from difficult conversations. I don't need to be an apologist for God or an apologist for the enlightenment movement. I just don't want innocent people in the Christian community to miss out on what could be a remarkable revelation about the way the human operating system works, one that is spreading throughout the world and providing those who understand it with a more helpful way to navigate even the most basic lifestyle in the 2020s and beyond.

Enriched again with the knowledge of the sinful nature and the way it infects our old mind, I began to see how the principles are such an effective way of navigating away from the patterns of the world and working with God's spirit in the renewal process.

As thought leaders in the Christian community, we have a responsibility to explore this opportunity, rather than trying to protect our young and old with mental health issues from our suspicious fears of a spirituality-based understanding that could bring them inner peace and open a special and personal relationship with Jesus.

## The Principles for Healing Spiritual Distress

Why is it that scripture, Church attendance, and prayer is NOT proving enough to save people from mental distress?

It's because we are all (many churches included) using the wrong psychological model and if we have the map upside down, we'll never find our way home.

If even in the Christian community we are using an out-of-date something-wrong mental model that it is unfit for purpose in a time of cultural change—and many of us also still live in a dualistic misunderstanding where God is in heaven—we are living out a life on earth separate from him.

## The Inside-Out Covenant

In the New Testament, the Apostle Paul writes that we need renewing of the mind, and this new mind heals the rift between God and humanity.

This is because it is God's gift to us, it's God's initiative, it's his New Covenant in Jesus, and anything that falls short of that truth is a not-truth, in other words, it's a lie, and a lie based on unbelief, that old legacy from the beginning of the human era, a legacy from the Garden of Eden, of rebellion, based on deception, leading the decay and death.

When we apply this outside-in understanding to Jesus's teaching in the Beatitudes, we find that they are impossible to live by because for one reason, we have the 'map' of life upside down, and for another reason, Jesus is explaining what life is like in the power of the Holy Spirit, not by a change of instructions.

We cannot *do* the Beatitudes, only God can, that's the point.

Just as we haven't understood the inside-out nature of the psychological human operating system, we haven't fully embraced God's newer inside-out covenant where His Holy Spirit entwines in our spirit, enlivens our soul, and communes with us in the private world of the mind.

For many, God is still outside, and we are acting in a way to please him to gain our reward.

Enlightenment truly came when God introduced Jesus to the world. God's plan was to redeem all creation but, as the parable of the sower describes, some seeds fall on stony ground, some fall on unresponsive ground, but some do fall on fertile soil and those people who have seen the inside-out nature of our enlightened state are more at peace and happier, irrespective of their religion.

### Religion or Spirituality?

Religion is outside in; God's New Covenant is inside out.

Humanistic psychology is outside in; principles psychology is inside out.

Humanistic spirituality needs effort and imagination. Biblical spirituality needs faith.

Part Two now explores how the inside-out revelation is inherent in the Bible.

# Part Two

# A Biblical Revelation

*Introduction.* As I was writing this book, I was pondering the question of how I could reconcile the principle-based spiritually driven psychology and the teaching of the Bible?

*Then it struck me so fundamentally that they both focus on the inside-out nature of human life and the way it plays out on planet Earth.*

*Part Two of this book concentrates on the biblical teaching of the inside-out New Covenant and the transition we must experience as the renewed mind's values emerge in our awareness and challenge the habitual mind's earthbound strategies, fighting to keep us in service to our habitual conditioning.*

*A lot of people talk about us being spiritual beings in a material world without having any idea what that might mean. Apparently, according to this idea, we are innocently 'trapped' in a world of 'form' but if that's the case, then that means there must be somewhere else where everything is ok, another world of not-form. This leads to duality, a sort of 'not great here, so it must be better there' operating model. Maybe that's where the misunderstanding of what heaven might be like came from, suggesting that one day we'll get 'up there' if we behave ourselves 'down here'.*

*A reasonable study of the Bible will disprove this idea as not grounded in the scriptures.*

*Unless we understand the implications of the original Satanic-influenced human rebellion against the creator God, we are working on misinformation. Even worse, if we don't even understand the inherent strategies of the earthbound, me-first mind that we have inherited from our ancestors, we will not appreciate how we have been consequently programmed and conditioned to navigate this material landscape like strangers in a wilderness.*

*It's little wonder that through our negative mind we see problems and challenges instead of solutions and opportunities.*

*We have to remind our earthbound mind that it needs to accept its spiritual nature. It's within our power to do this as long as we work with the Holy Spirit to empower and equip us to pay less attention to earthly things and more to heavenly things.*

*In other words, if we always do what we've always done, we'll always get what we've always got.*

*So the chapters in Part Two bring us more awareness of this different dimension of life, one that the Bible calls 'heaven' and Jesus refers to as an invisible Kingdom not of this world but equally created by God, a dimension of reality that has never gone away but one that we as humans have innocently chosen to ignore. We've consequently allowed the mind to calibrate to our senses to guide us to the extent that the material world is all that most of us are aware of.*

*The quality of life of this dimension is called 'eternal life'. For a lot of people, eternal life is either an everlasting version of this one, which might not be an attractive proposition at all, or a continuation of this one but with a bit more singing and Bible study on a Sunday morning.*

*Jesus displayed a vastly different type of life. A life of close communion with the God who re-adopts us into his family and gives us an inheritance in his Kingdom, evidenced by miracles, healings, raising of the dead, but during this time on earth, opposition and persecution from those who are yet to 'see the light'. To experience this quality of eternal life we don't need to go anywhere, travel the world, or meet a guru.*

*Eternal life is the life of the inside-out Kingdom.*

*This was seen by so-called enlightened people for many years before Jesus came on the scene and by many more since he left this stage to return to the source of all life.*

*Paradise wasn't lost, we just can't 'see' it because of the old, rebellious, me-first mind's obsession with the senses, so in this part of the book I will offer more pointers, but we all have the free will to decide if we want to put on inside-out spectacles. This is our choice.*

## The Biblical Revelation

*Our mind is where we communicate with God.*

*The Bible explains how this communication has been interrupted and how it can be restored.*

*The human mind has become infected with destructive patterns of thought leading to actions and behaviour that are destroying us and our home, planet earth.*

*Restoration of the communication between us and our creator, the source of life, requires a change of mind, a mind that operates on God's wavelength. God has made this mind available for everyone and has shown us in Jesus Christ where we will find it and how it brings freedom and restoration.*

*Jesus taught through a parable in the Bible about a man who found treasure buried in a field. When he found it, he hid it again, then sold all he had and bought that field.*

*This book is about both treasure and field. Both are discoverable for all of us because the treasure has never really been hidden, we've just been looking in the wrong part of the field.*

*The title of this book is An Inside-Out Revelation. Think of it as a guide to finding the treasure.*

*The field, in this instance, is what we call the mind, what I also refer to as our 'operating system'.*

*The hidden treasure is the Kingdom of God.*

*The Bible teaches us that in the hidden Kingdom of God there exists a different state of mind that reinstates our connection and relationship with God, the relationship that was lost way back at the start of the human era.*

*The account of the first humans helps us to understand how to restore this communication and letters of guidance are written in the New Testament by one of the most influential characters in God's plan of redemption. He is known as the Apostle Paul and wrote about this in his letters to the early Christian communities, providing them with the enlightening guidance they needed to find the Kingdom of God in their inner world.*

*In his letter entitled Romans, he stated, 'Do not conform to the pattern of this world but be transformed by the renewing of your mind,' 12:2 (NIV).*

*What is this renewal? How does it work, how can we get it and what will life look like when we have it?*

## Renewing the Mind

*To change our mind, we need to understand how the present one works, so that we can recognise the 'patterns of this world' and begin the transition.*

*Through the generations, the fallen mind (or, as I also refer to it, the old mind or the habitual mind), has been conditioned to operate independently from God, outside of the covenant of love and protection that God had established with the first humans.*

*The nature of that old mind shows itself so clearly in human behaviour and it hasn't changed in thousands of years of our history.*

*It shows itself in relationship breakdowns, in wars over land, in jealousy, hatred, judgement, and competition.*

*The sense of isolation and insecurity that all humans feel deep down is the treasure buried deep in our personal field calling out to us, 'Dig, dig!'*

*The reward for our digging is finding that recreation of our operating system is available through a new birth, awakening us to spiritual reality, one that brings us redemption, salvation, re-establishing the relationship as it was meant to be. As we are given this renewed mindset, our new navigation system is connected to a very different network, one that is broadcasting positive thoughts from a higher consciousness: a network of peace, love, joy, and infinite creativity.*

## The 'Spade' of Faith

*Our conundrum is that the old mind is not naturally spiritual, so it will not willingly support a mission to seek out something that is invisible, something beyond reason and intellectual logic. This is because it's obsessed with its earthbound reality, the material things of life.*

*The conundrum is that we cannot fully see the Kingdom of God until we have the renewed mind, and we don't fully get the renewed mind until we have seen the Kingdom of God.*

*There is a solution, however, because one of the tools God has provided for our mission is faith—faith that what we can't see exists.*

*Even with our old, sceptical mind we can see the effects of the Kingdom reflected in creation, albeit impurely, so that when we locate and install the renewed mind, we will know it's the Kingdom and it will feel like coming home.*

*The old mind will literally become a thing of memory.*

# Chapter Eight

# Preparing for Renewal

## Introduction

*This chapter explores further the need for us to renew our mind and brings in more of the biblical teaching on the subject, alongside the psychological strategies already considered in Part One.*

*Attempts to change the mind by therapeutic intervention or self-negotiation have proven generally ineffective up to now. I'm exposing the factual truth that despite our best efforts, the human mind seems to naturally operate from a state of fear and insecurity, creating in us an internal world of judgement and comparison. Self-sabotage and imposter syndrome are symptomatic and the behaviour that emerges from the strategies of this mind proves this to be true.*

*Now is the time that humanity must find a way to practically apply the solution to the problem of the mind.*

*From a biblical perspective, the solution has been staring us in the face for two thousand years so now that a huge shift is taking place in the spiritual realm of our human experience, there are more opportunities opening up.*

*However, what I'm proposing in this book isn't evolution, it's an inside-out revolution.*

*I wrote this chapter following a summer course that I ran at Kingsland Church in Colchester, Essex on practical renewal of the mind.*

*Seasoned Christians found that learning about the psycho–spiritual, inside-out nature of the mind helped them to understand how we can break the habitual patterns of thought and so hear fresh revelation and insight from God's Holy Spirit.*

## Psychological Breakthrough or Spiritual Awakening

Many of the clients that refer to me have faith in a God of some sort, or at least believe in a creative universal energy of some kind so, as a mental health professional, I have been particularly keen to understand why even people of faith still struggle with worry, stress, anxiety, depression, and suicidal thoughts about themselves and their everyday life situations.

For those who believe and trust God is real and relevant, the Bible's accounts of God's influence promise a very different way of life, a deeper understanding of who, what, and where we are, enabling us to cast off many of our cares, possibly even giving up worrying as a pointless exercise.

But still the question remained. Why do those of us whose minds have an element of awakening still seem to be in bondage to our old patterns of behaviour?

## Living in Reality

It seems so prevalent in our lives that we spend huge amounts of time and energy trying to get somewhere that we think will be better than where we are now.

For years I searched the theories, the philosophies, and the religions to find the key to this conundrum. Very few people seemed to be happy with what they had, always wanting something else, something different.

In an attempt to stay present, to heal this 'better there' rift, I practised the techniques passed down by the giants of psychology and philosophy that had gone before me, but without the level of success I had hoped for.

I had undoubtedly experienced the power of God in my personal life, but was I restricting God in my professional practice, preferring not to impose Him on my clients (unless they asked)? And as a result, was I compromising myself both personally and ethically?

I have a duty to provide my clients with the best help I can, but I realised that I had persuaded myself that they might be offended by the message of the Bible.

How could I point them to the spiritual reality of life? A spiritual reality that was grounded in reality, a deep foundation rather than in the uncertain instability of the worldly system.

Then, in 2009, I learnt of the new spirituality-based form of psychology that had been uncovered in the 1970s but was growing in popularity and efficacy. This is where I began to see the benefits of a spiritually inclusive model that might be the way to introduce God into the discussion about mind, especially as this new discovery also had an innate logic and common sense.

I saw a spirituality relevant to everyday life, work, and relationships, one that saw spirit as formless energy. How could anyone possibly object or be offended by that?

## Mind Consciousness and Thought

As we've explored in Part One, this understanding reveals the mind's operating principles: consciousness (or awareness) and thought which are not theoretical but intelligent, spiritual energies that we all use to create our personal perception of the world, moment to moment, from the inside out.

I switched the focus of my practice from the theory-based humanistic approaches to one grounded in these spiritual principles because this gave me the opportunity to bring a spiritual dimension into my work, while respecting my client's own preferences and beliefs.

This seemed to be the ideal direction for my practice. A spiritual solution to a psychological problem. It seemed that I could provide clients with a route to awakening without having them understand the Bible.

## Wrong Direction?

Personally, this decision had the opposite effect on my wellbeing. To the denigration of my practice and my own life foundations I soon learnt that for me, teaching a spirituality without Bible foundations was like trying to hold fast running water in my hands. The more 'spirituality' I pursued, the more I felt a growing emptiness that warned me that the direction in which I was heading was sacrificing something vital.

The emptiness and isolation I was experiencing was ruining my ability to reason and I lost my connection to reality, spending hours in pointless meditations and silence practices.

I started to enquire of online gurus and subscribed to YouTube New Age philosophers, even though for many years I had known that human wisdom and philosophy isn't the way to the love and adoption into God's family.

Spiritual darkness was upon me. I was alone and very lost.

## Wake Up Sleeper

Then one day it hit me like a ton of bricks!

I literally woke up and recognised that there is one common cause and one common cure for the human condition that is the root of our lostness, isolation, insecurity, and fear of the future.

We need to renew our mind and how we go about that is an inside-out revelation.

Ironically, that revelation resulted in me returning to the source that gave me a lifeline from my own depression and suicidal thoughts—the Bible.

More precisely, my search has come home to rest on the best piece of advice I've ever received in my personal or professional life: 'Do not conform to the patterns of this world but be transformed by the renewing of your mind.'

This was like a voice from my distant past. In my wilderness I was journeying farther away from God and so I had to ask myself a big question; Can we live God's way without God's love and power?

## Travelling Home

Through focusing on my circumstances, my problems, I'd lost contact with my guide and, like Pinocchio, I'd been tempted to go to the fair and I'd left my Jiminy Cricket outside.

The fair was full of bright lights and fame, plenty of opportunities for my ego to regain the upper hand in the battle for my soul.

I realised that even God's porch light is brighter than the world's floodlights. Even though I'd wandered far from home, he's always left a light burning for me.

I'm no longer compromising my own belief in the biblical God who is my personal treasure but, because I've experienced both routes to enlightenment—humanistic philosophy and biblical spirituality—I knew deep down which one was truly home.

## Jesus the Gatekeeper

So now I feel qualified to write about what I've found, because I believe that the direction of travel for anyone seeking spiritual enlightenment must inevitably bring us all face to face with Jesus, who is the expression of the creator God, the source that we are all seeking.

This is why the first part of this book was offering, in love and hope, freedom from the habitual patterns of the me-first mind with the option of the new psycho–spiritual paradigm of the Three Principles.

Whether or not the reader wants to accept God's plan of redemption and renewal of the mind, whether they feel it is relevant in their everyday life, it's possible to break the patterns of the world and be free of habitual thinking. But philosophy still doesn't fully address the human need for unconditional love and adoption that only Jesus Christ can provide.

## The Field Illuminated

So let's explore the history and legacy of the mind according to the Bible, showing us more about both the cause of the human condition and routes to the cure.

To find the treasure first we need to locate the field.

## The Bible's Map of Life

The universal map that the Bible provides is true for all of us, inclusive of all humanity, but with special relevance to the community of believers (the Church) as we work together to get the best from the treasure and point others to its location.

The 'field' is revealed once we turn from the outside-in pursuit of meaning and realise that we must journey inwardly, into the spirit, where the soul of our individuality is waiting for refreshment.

Enlightenment is like floodlights that, when switched on, illuminate the field and we can begin to realise that we are getting nearer to our treasure.

In the psycho–spiritual enlightenment route, we are more likely to be working individually, so we will still be mainly navigating from the psychological map that we have personally created from our own life experience.

## We Create Our Map of the World

As we travel through life and experience events, we make a personal map of the world. It is not the map of the whole world, but our personal map (see the chapter on God's satnav and algorithms).

The personal map cannot possibly contain all the information we need to make the most informed decisions and what's more worrying, is that the personal navigation system is still grounded in the old mind which can subtly take us further away from our inner peace and ultimately further from God.

As we see in the chapter on God's original design, God created the first human from the 'dust of the earth' so in today's language, we could say we are carbon-based.

God breathed his spirit into Adam's earthly body, and he became a living soul.

The problem was that due to the rebellion of sin that already existed in nature following Satan's rebellion, these three parts—spirit, body, and soul—are working in a conflict that the unrenewed mind cannot manage. It's like owning a new Rolls Royce with the management system of a 1980s Skoda.

This is because the earth body is downward-oriented and focuses on home being in the material realm, whereas the spirit is upward, from God, and focuses on the heavenly realm.

The soul is the individual, trapped between earth and heaven, the Devil on one shoulder and the angel on the other, if you get the metaphor?

So when the renewed mind is calibrated primarily upwards it will lead us that way because the renewed mind is managed by God's operating system, the Holy Spirit, and that is God in person, inside us, in our mind and our heart.

## Holy Spirit

Just prior to the end of Jesus's mission on earth, before he returned to the Father, he promised his disciples that it was better for them that he was going because then the Holy Spirit, aka the Spirit of truth, would come, live in them, guide them, and provide all the power and wisdom they would need.

Because the old mind is, by nature, rebellious it will resist the spirit of truth and pursue its own truth and so there is often resistance. The old mind isn't going to willingly lead itself to a place of its own destruction. Turkeys for Christmas?

I hope that this book helps point you to God's universal map so you can find his treasure and, when you hold that treasure in your hand, in your mind, and in your heart, you will find the peace that passes all human understanding through a renewed mind, the key to eternal life.

## Coming Home

This journey home is illustrated in the biblical parable of the lost son who chooses to return to his father and the family home. Having taken his inheritance early and had a great time in the world, he ended up losing all his money and sleeping with the pigs. So the young adventurer heads back home, expecting to receive a cold reception from his father and older brother who stayed behind. Instead, the father sees his young son coming and rushes out to meet him, welcomes him, and feeds and dresses him. The older brother is jealous, but the father puts him right. Everyone who chooses to make coming home their priority in life will be welcomed and even if we choose a more circuitous route, the God of all creation is always secretly, lovingly, guiding us home.

So I'm presenting you with a route to finding the invisible Kingdom of God inside through the teachings of the Bible, but I'm also acknowledging that there is an alternative route available to us, a route through awakening of the human spirit through a different form of spirituality-based psychology.

Either way, the journey is inward, and the revelation awaits, inside.

## Can the Church Accept the Human Enlightenment Route?

Every one of us, even Jesus himself, has been born into a world that carries the legacy of fear and insecurity handed down genetically and spiritually from our first parents right back at the beginning of the human era.

In scripture, it is clearly stated that God's Kingdom is not of this world and in that other-worldly dimension he calls heaven, the cure doesn't lay in what we see around us but in a renewed mind, operating internally.

This renewed mind is like an upgrade for your computer, and it is ours through faith in Jesus Christ.

The Bible states that a renewed mind is needed to connect with the heavenly realm because the old mind has been honed and sharpened to navigate in this fallen, dying, corrupt world.

If the Apostle Paul wrote in his New Testament letters to the new Church communities about not conforming to patterns of the world two thousand years ago, how ingrained must those patterns be by now?

Equally it is important to understand what patterns existed in those days, in the decades following Jesus's resurrection and how that supernatural meeting between Jesus and Paul on the road to Damascus instigated God's plan for redemption of all people through a most unlikely human.

## The Mind Before Renewal

The pre-renewed or 'old' mind displays what the Bible calls our sinful nature, which was founded on rebellious lies and deception emanating from Satan's mission to disrupt God's plan. Satan, who is referred to in the Bible as 'the father of lies' and 'the ruler of this world', corrupted the dwelling place of the first humans to play out his rebellion against the creator God, by deceiving humanity and persuading our forebears that he could open their eyes so that they (and consequently us) could all be like God (Genesis 1–3).

Little wonder our minds have become so negative, no wonder we feel lost, alone, and fearful from as far back as we can remember. Little wonder we cling to our earthly parents, for some form of security, even into our own old age. Little wonder that we persuade ourselves that we will be happy when we eventually find meaning and success and often, even if we do, we still don't know who or what we really are.

Little wonder our lives are full of worry, stress, anxiety, depression, and suicidal thoughts.

We have lost our inheritance, connection with our creator, but God has opened up ways for us to be reunited to the source of all that we need.

An upgrade is available, would you like to install?

To appreciate this, we need to renew our operating system.

God has provided the upgrade. We need to download it by faith and install it through actions.

The renewed mind is a quiet, peaceful, content but immensely creative space which enables us to produce the fruit of the Holy Spirit.

Calibration from the old mind to that new mind is the purpose of this book.

To assist in the recalibration, I will still use various visual models which appeared in Part One, and more in Part Three, by which we can observe the workings of the old mind, integrate the new mind and when the time is right for everyone, make the switch.

## Like Learning a New Language

I've spoken with many people who have learnt to speak a new language but still retain their native tongue as their first language.

For example, for an English speaker who has learnt Italian, my question for them would be, 'Do you still think in English and translate in your mind before you speak in Italian?' The answer, I've found, often varies depending on the time the individual has been practising the new language. Calibration varies according to time, motive, effort, commitment, and skill.

In fact, thinking about thinking can be a roundabout that can have us becoming dizzy with 'what-ifs' and 'how comes'.

We think, we are thinking creatures, it's in our DNA, in our structure and the creative power of thought is what we use to create the reality we experience.

When we think, we use language. When we talk to ourselves, we must understand what we are saying. So how did thought work out before we learnt our native language? How did we think when we were two years old? Well, the fact is that we can't remember when we were two years old because we hadn't learnt how to do that. Thinking is a learnt behaviour and without understanding the power it holds, incorrect use of thought can unleash devastating pain and suffering on us.

Thinking starts with language so that is probably why we only remember experiences from a time when we could talk to ourselves, give meaning to what we experienced and started to use thought to programme our brain, create memories, and then become conscious of them.

Once we could talk to ourselves in our minds, we began to overwrite the childlike innocence of our innate wellbeing, our birthright, with that old legacy mind of fear, isolation, competition, judgement, and comparison.

Jesus said that to enter the Kingdom of Heaven we must become like little children.

Now we know why. Little children accept what their father says and do it, until a time comes when they learn about rebellion. Jesus loved his Father and said that he only did what he saw his Father do. That's the point. The renewed mind is not rebellious, unless it is renewed through humanistic psychological principles that deny Jesus as the Son of God.

The innocence we were all born with becomes infected by the learning the behaviour of a society infected by the rebellious mind, and our first few years of life often become a transition from joy to confusion and fear.

So that old mind has had many years of conditioning and takes time to recalibrate, to accept any new experience, in a different way, stepping aside to allow the new operating system that space it needs, space to create fundamental changes in our attitudes towards life and the people around us.

Initially there might well be a clunky internal translation as then old narratives are replaced by a more natural process, until our new 'language' of love and kindness becomes second nature as our thinking, Speaking, and actions align and calibrate.

Operating the new mind might take us a while or maybe it'll happen supernaturally in a moment. In his New Testament letters, Paul tells how he clearly struggled with his transition and his honesty about it should encourage us, especially as he is seen as the prototype model of the Christian, the first of his self-titled 'new creation in Christ', perhaps the first truly born-again believer.

As far as I know, in his time on earth, Paul didn't have any working illustrative models of the mind but nowadays we are used to having useful illustrations, guides, hacks, and programmes so I'm going to provide some guidance that has helped me and countless clients to get a handle on renewing that wibbly-wobbly, invisible mystery that we call the mind into something truly glorious.

We need to get a clear understanding of how the old mind works so that we can be conscious of navigating the transition to the new one, and therefore complete the recalibration without causing too much damage to ourselves and others along the way.

God has granted us something very, very special to help us with the transition and it's called grace.

If we choose to follow the humanistic approach it can reveal a depth of human spirit that can empower some of the greatest endeavours the world has ever seen. Great industry, medicine, travel, and unbelievable feats of strength have been achieved through human inspiration and God in grace allows such advancements to bless and assist human growth.

However, what is there at the end of that journey?

The Bible warns us of three illustrations of the fallen mind in operation: the lust of the eye, (jealousy), the lust of the flesh (sexual immorality), and the pride of life (endeavours that glorify human achievement).

If our human endeavours reflect these motivations, we are still in the wrong field and the treasure we unearth there will lack the attributes of the renewed mind: love, peace, joy, thanksgiving, and eternal life.

Please don't allow yourself to be condemned by this. Jesus said that he never came into the world to condemn it but came because God so loved the world, he wants to save it.

Allow yourself grace as we now take the signpost to the narrower path that, for many people, turns out to be the most important journey of their lives: the route into the inside-out revelation that allows entry the wonderland that is the Kingdom of heaven.

# Chapter Nine

## God's Original Design and the Human Rebellion

*The Bible does just what it is supposed to do: Outline the history and future of mankind and show how through faith in Jesus Christ, one can receive eternal life.' Internet quote, origin unknown.*

### Introduction

*In 1988 I had a life-changing experience. At that time, I didn't believe in the God of the Bible, but I somehow knew that life must have a deeper meaning. I had been searching for that meaning even before I was a teenager so it was a relief, and a bit like finding hidden treasure, when, upon reading C.S. Lewis's book* Mere Christianity *that I realised this faith potentially offered me a much deeper spiritual experience than Sunday school had ever suggested.*

*As I hadn't had any spiritual guidance from my parents, apart from an hour at Sawyers Hall Lane Chapel Sunday school in Brentwood, Essex, I reckoned that I was free to make my own choice regarding religion, and so I decided, at 33 years of age, that if any part of the Bible was true, as C.S. suggested, then all of it should be true and I would hang my hat on that peg, settle in and take the ride to life that was on offer.*

*Thirty-three years later, that decision has led me to experience the most incredible life journey, one full of unspeakable miracles and huge challenges, and I have no regrets.*

*This is why now, as a psychotherapist helping people tame their own minds that are so unruly and stubborn, I take even more seriously the Bible account of how that unruly mind came about and how it has become the cause of humanity's pain.*

*Here is a summary, but I ask you please to read again the book of Genesis and see what the Holy Spirit shows you, because this is time for us to take back our spiritual legacy and live, fully human.*

## Creation

In the Bible account, called Genesis, humanity's firstborn, Adam and Eve, are created by God to be his companions. They are given a safe place to start their life purpose of populating the earth with more like themselves.

In the background of this creation story is the legacy of some vast spiritual rebellion led by one of God's created spirit beings, Lucifer. His rebellion and the ensuing 'war in heaven' clearly seems to still be playing out. So we find Lucifer exiled from heaven and present in Eden during these early stages of the human era on earth, the created, material realm.

In the scriptures, we are not told too much about this conflict between God and Lucifer, and maybe too much detail might be a distraction from the Bible's primary message of human redemption, but in Revelation Chapter 12 there is an account of a war in heaven, so please read this and make your own conclusions.

So Lucifer, now renamed as Satan (meaning the accuser), clearly sees an opportunity to continue to strengthen his rebellion and, fuelled by his ambition to be superior to God, by his spirit he inhabits one of the beasts that God had created, the serpent. Disguised as the serpent, he is able to hide out in Eden with Adam and Eve.

## The Two Trees

God had built into the creation the ability for his humans to be free to make their own decisions so to enable this, and as part of his wider plan to rid his creation of the harmful effects of the rebellion (which the Bible calls sin), the trees in the garden had fruit that produced different spiritual characteristics and powers that would guide the early humans with God's wisdom.

One particular tree was called the tree of life and its fruit contained the wisdom of God. Another tree was the tree of the knowledge of good and evil. God's instructions to Adam and Eve were not to eat the fruit of that tree, otherwise there would be serious consequences for them and their offspring—death!

Lucifer must have been aware of this somehow and so, disguised as the serpent, he used his higher awareness to trick Eve. Eve innocently listened to his temptations as he cast doubt on God's trustworthiness and she, assuming that he was wise and that he had wisdom that would give her enlightenment and with it, special knowledge, took his guidance instead.

She listened to the serpent who persuaded her that she could be 'like God' if she ate from the tree of the knowledge of good and evil. It was a tempting offer and so she took the challenge and persuaded Adam to do the same.

## Rebellion

Instantly, their eyes were opened to be able to interpret good and evil, but the act of disobedience caused separation from God, because once they knew evil, they had knowledge of the implications of their actions. Realising their mistake, they covered their shame and guilt, hiding from God in the bushes, covering their nakedness with fig leaves.

At that initial moment of rebellion, Adam and Eve, our first ancestors, were given notice to quit their paradise home of Eden, that safe place where they shared in open fellowship with God.

Outside of Eden, they had to use their best endeavours to find a way of navigating a life of separation from God's wisdom. They, and consequent generations of humanity, were forced to develop a personal survival mindset, an intellectual capacity to navigate life outside the Garden of Eden in a world where different rules and laws apply, a world where the knowledge of good and evil causes the human mind to overthink, to worry, to create anxiety, stress, depression, and suicidal thoughts.

The legacy of leaving Eden are these destructive patterns of thought and behaviour embedded in our operating system that are the root cause of all human suffering.

That mind-without-God is sometimes referred to as 'fallen' because it can never achieve the dimension of awareness, the heights of joy, love, and peace that freely come to us from God's nature. This fall from grace has left humanity insecure, fearful, lost, and feeling guilty, spiritually far removed from a loving, personal relationship with God the creator.

## Disconnected

Until we realise the impact of losing our connection with God, we will not understand why we feel lost, isolated, and insecure.

If we are still in the dark about our spiritual source we are like orphans searching planet earth for the home we lost but once we have the inside-out revelation, we realise we have been looking in the wrong direction.

Looking outside ourselves, scouring the world for our Eden, our promised land, we look for it in our external activities, in relationships and possessions, but we are looking in the wrong direction.

As children, we are taken to the playground where swings and slides provide a sort of safe place for us to play. For the rest of our lives, many of us continue to seek the equivalent of that playground, our personal Eden.

In the Bible, the name for Eden became 'heaven' and to this day, Satan continues to put doubt in our fallen minds, tricking us into thinking it's a distant dream that has nothing to do with our lives on planet earth. We can only reach it by being good until the day we die and even then, we have no idea if we'll qualify for entry.

Jesus referred to our destination as the Kingdom of God and he taught that it was inside us, which means that we already have it and that every physical step we take takes us further from heaven.

## Why Did God Allow This?

That question is asked by most humans even to this day. I hear it all the time.

Why did God allow evil in the Garden of Eden and why does it still exist now, why didn't he just wipe it out? All the time we witness evil people, evil acts, and evil outcomes.

## Trust

You know what it's like when you doubt someone, you lose trust in them.

We have lost trust in God, and fallen into a spiritual gap between God and Satan, into a vacuum as deep as a black hole.

Consequently, we look to replace that deep sense of lostness in the world of material form.

What is our metaphorical fig leaves now? How do we cover our nakedness and isolation from God? Busyness, activity, building empires, gathering possessions, and money?

The Kingdom of God is within.

# Chapter Ten

# God's Plan of Redemption

*For God so loved the world that he gave his one and only son. John 3:16 (NIV).*

## Introduction

*As I was writing this book it struck me that the collection of ancient writings that make up the Bible have been chosen because they 'hang together' to form a complete narrative that explains what's going on right now, in this 'human era'. There are many wonderful and thought-provoking philosophical writings beyond the covers of the Bible that ponder the meaning of life, but the difference is that the Bible explains it.*

*Before we look at various aspects of God's redemption plan in more detail, in this chapter is my quick take on the whole story, just to set the scene. But first something about the various translations of the Bible.*

## Bible References

I'm going to use Bible references, but because there are so many translations available, I've used the English Standard Version (ESV), the New International Version (NIV), the New Living Translation (NLT) and The Passion Translation (TPT).

I invite you to read any Bible references in your favourite Bible translation, and then choose a different version, one you're not used to. In fact, read as many versions as you want to because this is your decision, your free will, your time, your life with God in Christ (and it helps with pattern interruption!).

Enjoy it, that is what God intends for you.

Read and listen to the Holy Spirit. Let God show you what you've never seen before.

My aim is to focus on the scriptural teachings that support the principles operating in the mind, the principles we can call thought and consciousness, but I also need to include references to heart, soul, and spirit These are terms integral to the scriptural understanding of our human operating system; I have also found these terms can be interchangeable at times depending on the translation that I'm reading.

It's worth bearing in mind the prevailing understanding of how a human being was interpreted when Bible passages were written. This way we can understand that the word 'spirit' is a more modern term for 'breath' and so 'Holy Spirit' is 'holy breath', and is the breath of God himself.

There isn't space in this book to investigate such depth of language but for New Testament quotes I have favoured the Greek/English parallel because I wanted the words I use to be as close to the original Greek as possible.

There are versions that are based on word-for-word translations and others based on interpretation of the meaning and, for me, The Passion Translation offers a rich experience of this and so I've used this to bring balance to the message.

I would rather not be prescriptive as to which version you use, but prefer that you use various translations, one with which you are familiar and comfortable, but keep your options open and you might find at times that where I've used a translation that refers to 'thought' or 'mind', the one you prefer maybe uses the word 'heart' or 'soul'.

I hope we can agree that the importance is in what is behind the words, the message itself, and this isn't the place for discussions about ethics of translation, as long as we see the truth in the message to make a fair assessment of the principles as taught in scripture.

## In the Beginning, God

I'm going to start at the beginning, in Genesis, and the account of the creation of humanity.

In Genesis Chapter 3 we have what is referred to as 'the fall'. Adam and Eve disobeyed God and aligned with Lucifer, a spirit being exiled from God's presence as the result of a war in heaven before the human story begins.

God then shows his kind and loving nature even in the face of their actions as he allows the whole of creation to fall with Adam and Eve, so that they wouldn't die straight away but be given a chance for redemption. They would live in a separate reality (dimension) from God that allowed them to survive but toil, in pain and suffering, using their soulish personalised mind. Their 'independent from God' operating system wasn't honed and practised in the environment of a safe garden world but in a barren wilderness, a separate dimension from Eden, one that they could tend for themselves. But, as God promised, it wouldn't be easy.

This shows God's infinite care for humans, that there is always a plan of redemption running through the ages, but also there is his plan for the annihilation of Satan's rebellion, who was, by choice, also trapped in this fallen reality (dimension).

So, the rest of the Bible tells us of God progressing his plan for the redemption of humans and the whole of creation through covenant agreements.

In his love for his people his plan is to rescue and eventually bring humanity into a new world through the new nature in Christ.

The final covenant described in the Bible is contained in the New Testament. God changes his operating model from an outside-in law maker to an inside-out spiritual guide.

It's a brilliant and totally loving plan.

It's the time we are now living in, called the 'Church' age.

## Exposing the Fallen Mind Operating Today

As we explore God's plan, I invite you to reflect back on Part One of this book and the event cycle, the overthinking progression, and the conscious levels.

Do these models help to expose the old mind's strategies and help us calibrate to the new mind?

To survive outside of God's presence, humanity has developed a way of using God's gifts of thought and consciousness to navigate a dangerous environment. We have learnt to use these principles to create our experience of life but in doing so we each create our own reality.

This unrenewed mind creates separation, not communion. We think me first and our focus is naturally about personal survival.

## Glimpses of the New Mind

As I explained in Part One, there are hints of the renewed mind available in our rebellious nature and great works of human kindness show through in glimpses. However, if we explore the roots of endeavours such as the education system, abolition of slavery, and acts of philanthropy, God's light is shining in the hearts of those who have been the movers and the shakers.

With the renewed mind, a new way of thinking and a different quality of consciousness is available and we can begin to enjoy the 'quality of eternal life' that God has for us all.

## Reversing the Curse

Jesus was baptised in water immediately after which the Holy Spirit descended on him and a voice 'from heaven' announced that God the father was well pleased with his son.

After this, the Spirit led Jesus into the wilderness and there he was tempted by Satan, just as Adam had been, but this time Jesus didn't obey and thus Satan's power was overcome and Jesus took on the role of a 'second Adam' breaking the power of rebellion and reversing the curse from Eden.

## Full Restoration is Still to Come

With the beginning of the process of redemption Jesus establishes the next stage of God's programme and the 'church age' begins where all humans have the choice to accept Jesus and are spiritually born again through the Holy Spirit but full completion of this plan will not occur until Jesus returns.

However, in the meantime we have the renewed mind and the power of the Holy Spirit to manifest the inside out Kingdom on the earth from day to day, bringing life and light into the darkness of the rebellious, sinful world system which still manifests the legacy of the fall.

## Are the Principles from God?

Are these principles of thought and consciousness, the operating powers in the mind, God inspired, man-made, or Satanic trickery? Or are they simply an upgrade for the old operating system we need to navigate the fallen dimension independently, or are they an evolutionary gift from the God of the Bible, the father/creator, to move us nearer to him?

I propose that the key to this is the mission of Jesus Christ.

If the principles are a revolutionary key to establishing Jesus's Kingdom of Heaven on Earth, did he teach this?

After Jesus's death, resurrection, and ascension, did his servant Paul, in the power of the Holy Spirit, teach this?

Does God use Satan, who is trapped in this fallen world through his own choice following his rebellion against the creator, to bring humans back to himself? Satan is willing and able to act out of his totally sinful rebellious nature, while God is unable to do this as He has no sin.

Maybe Satan is God's Rottweiler, chained but still able to snarl and threaten with bared teeth and stinky breath?

God had already provided for this outcome and included a space or reality outside of Eden, maybe one that wasn't yet cultivated but was barren?

God is such a being that he can 'send his spirit', which seems to be his creative energy but is actually the third person of the Godhead, into this enemy territory to effect changes through the redeemed and regenerated Church.

## War in Heaven, Still Played Out on Earth?

Genesis 3 sets out the war between the serpent (Satan) and the woman (Eve, created as the producer of God's offspring).

So God now enables fallen man to regenerate through Jesus's death, resurrection and ascension, and the release of the Holy Spirit into the fallen dimension through regenerated humans, as shown in the character and activities of Paul and his followers, called Christians, who form the Church or 'bride of Christ'.

Jesus refers to the Church as His bride. Paul refers to Christians as being 'in Christ'. That is how entwined and entangled Jesus and his followers are during this era of the human age.

So now we will journey in more detail through some of the major aspects of God's plan and the human response.

## 1. Original Creation

Read Genesis 1 and 2 carefully, with an open mind, noting everything that is different from your preconceived ideas and concepts. I've been reading the Bible for half my life and when I researched it with a clear mind for this book, fresh aspects of the creation account have enlightened me to understand the reason why we humans act like we do. The need for the inside-out revelation became crystal-clear.

When reading this, please focus on the nature of the trees and the fruit of the two main trees, and the part they play in programming our mind to manifest fruit through our actions.

The trees in the garden were within reach of the humans. They didn't need a ladder to reach the fruit, so the trees weren't tall trees by implication.

They were fruit trees and fruit trees offer pickings.

Note how, for you, a fresh reading of the beginning of the human age can bring enlightenment as to how the so-called human condition was embedded and has manifested since.

Any interesting observations? What do you think?

How have perversions of the Word of God and misunderstandings of the message it brings weakened the impact on the underlying story of human history?

What are the practical implications of the fall and the redemption plan for life today?

For me, the images and revelations that struck me most were these:

The Lord God walking in the garden in the cool of the evening.

Adam being created outside of Eden and then placed in the garden, meaning that Eden must have been planted before Adam was put there.

Rivers flowed from Eden irrigating the surrounding land, so even thought it was a barren land, God still provided irrigation.

God offered Adam all the earlier creations before Eve as potential companions, but none were suitable as a true companion for him, so God created his companion, woman, from part of the man himself.

The serpent would have been one of the creatures that Adam had rejected as his companion.

There's nothing like a serpent scorned!

## 2. The Fall

Carefully read Genesis Chapter 3.

The serpent was one of the 'beasts' that the Lord had offered Adam as a companion!

Satan influenced Eve via the serpent, that was how Satan was able to be physically present in the garden because God had created him, as Lucifer, as a being of light, a spirit.

## 3. Original Sin (Rebellion)

Original disobedience of Eve and Adam as they rebelled against God's plan leads to enactment of the penalty for sin (rebellion) which is death. Initially they are banned from the garden and must make their way in the rest of the earth. God promises them it won't be easy but already he has a plan.

The 'curse of death' is not just for Adam but his offspring too, and this is shown in the subsequent account of Cain and his offspring. Expansion was immediate and violent.

## 4. Consequences and Implications

Read Genesis 4–6.

Man's self-centred legacy mind is designed and calibrated for sole survival in the land beyond Eden.

That mind is now fully operational in the unregenerated 'old' version of the human which carries inside the ticking timebomb of a death sentence like a great cloud of guilt and shame.

We can see the evidence through history and in present times.

In biblical language, the fruit of the tree of the knowledge of good and evil and the ability to be 'like God' is the manifesting act arising from the thought and act. Because it's the wrong God whose likeness we are reflecting.

The story unfolds and very quickly the traits of self-first, competition, deceit, lies, and mistrust infect human actions to the degree that self-destruction is rife, but God steps in with an attempt to clean up with a great flood.

The fallen mind is the soil in which the tree is planted; the thoughts, feelings, and action is the fruit.

The acts arising from the thought patterns of the unregenerate mind are indisputable evidence that the legacy mind still operates by default in all humans born of the flesh (See Jesus's teaching on being born again).

## 5. Old Mind

Read Romans 7–8.

Paul clearly sets out the problem of the old mind and the solution of the new mind with its vastly different thought patterns.

He tells from personal experience how the old mind is still at work in him to keep him aware of sin, the legacy based on serpent's lies that he carries, even after meeting the ascended Jesus himself.

The old mind can be cruel, it's a machine, it works on habits, routines, and programmes and needs to be supernaturally dealt the death blow that only being 'in Christ' can achieve.

This is why there are many therapeutic methods and theories that are offered but will only serve to keep us locked in its web of manipulation, domination, and control.

God's plan is that the old mind was crucified with Christ but each of us have to accept it and act on it by faith.

## 6. Redemption Plan

There are excellent summary accounts of God's redemption plan in the book of Acts, and they are addressed to very different audiences from the people of Israel, the Jewish authorities, philosophers, and non-believing pagans.

Read Acts 2, 16–38, which is the account of Peter teaching Jews that God accepts Gentiles too, that the plan of redemption is for everyone.

Read Acts 7, which is the account of Stephen's address to the High Priest and martyrdom for blasphemy.

Read Acts 10, 34–63 where Paul preaches to the household of a Gentile Roman centurion.

Read Acts 17 v 16 where Paul teaches the philosophers about the true meaning of life.

Read Acts 26, which is the Paul's defence account of his own conversion from teacher of the law to freedom in Christ.

All these accounts set out the choice that God has clearly offered humans, the choice between the old and new way, death or life. That's free will one hundred per cent of the time.

The two trees! The choice.

## 7. The Law Covenants

It's interesting to make a comparison between the old, outside-in, something-wrong psychology (change your circumstances, change your feelings) and God's covenants with Abraham and Moses through commandments, which stressed an outside-in set of rules.

However, the covenants were still based on personal love between God and His chosen ambassadors on earth and the law was given for the leaders to keep the tribes in order and as healthy and co-ordinated as possible for such a rebellious group of people.

God called Abram to move to a new location before he gave him the law covenant by which to live. Abram was called before the law which was given as a loving guide for creating a new caring community, a family.

Abram become Abraham (the H represents the breath of God, a forerunner to the Holy Spirit given to all 'in Christ' under the New Covenant) and he was obedient and in that covenant God blessed him because of the faith he acted out.

God called Moses and gave him the outside-in commandments, that were based on 'thou shall nots', so God was separating Moses and his people from Egypt with different ways of life.

How have even the Ten Commandments been trivialised, perverted into superstition at best?

The unregenerated mind cannot resist the temptation to break these commandments due to the inherent rebellion built into the nature of the sinful mind.

With the Ten Commandments, God was showing Moses how the fallen mind operated and asked him to help God's people begin to change their minds, but the nature of sin is so powerful that outside-in methods just didn't cut the mustard.

After prophesying the change to come, God fulfilled the law of life through the Word of life.

New Covenant commandments work from the inside-out and, although they are still our choice, then God joins us in deep personal fulfilment of all his promises to us.

## 8. Re-rebellion

Read any of Paul's letters on this. Romans contains his best writing on the difference between the old and new covenants but once we see that all the covenants are based on love and grace, we can relax into the great news that God has our back, whatever we've done, and Paul himself is the best example of that.

In Romans 6 verse 17, Paul writes, 'But thanks be to God that, though you used to be slaves to sin, you have come to obey from your heart the pattern of teaching that has now claimed your allegiance,' (NIV). God's grace is the greatest interrupter of the old patterns of the world as he teaches us new patterns that no longer conform to the rebellious nature.

What is the definition of not conforming? It is a person who does not conform to prevailing ideas or practices in their behaviour or views.

When we conform to God's New Covenant agreement, we are no longer conforming to the prevailing ideas of the world. We are rebelling against the world.

We are cancelling the Satanic rebellion by rebelling against it.

The inside-out revelation is a rebellious revolution based on love and truth.

## 9. Outside-In

This is where I get so excited about the inside-out nature of our experience. Whether we are lining our life up with the Word of God or a universal spiritual concept, we are amid a true revelation in the understanding of the human experience.

No longer do we need to fall for the misunderstanding that circumstances and other people are responsible for our feelings, or that we are individual strangers wandering as victim of circumstances in a strange land. Technically, our experience of life is from within our mind and Jesus taught clearly that God's Kingdom is within, and that is the focus of our efforts.

So, we can flow with the switch from the outside-in misunderstanding and in every sense become fully awake, fully aligned with life as it works right now.

The greatest pattern to break is the outside-in misunderstanding of how we experience life and the outside-in interpretation of imposed law.

## 10. Prophecy of the Inside-Out Kingdom

John the Baptist immersed repentant believers in water for cleansing, but he foretold of someone else who would baptise (immerse) in fire: Matthew 3:11 'I baptise you with water for repentance, but he who is coming after me is mightier than I, whose sandals I am not worthy to carry. He will baptise you with the Holy Spirit and fire.' (ESV.)

The fire, the Holy Spirit, dwells inside a person's operating system: the mind and the heart.

Jesus carried the authority to breathe the Holy Spirit. He breathes on the disciples before he sent them out on mission and, according to the Gospel accounts, on the cross, he breathed and gave his spirit.

The internal power of the Holy Spirit changes our minds and hearts from the inside, the very place where our experience of everyday life is processed.

Every human being experiences life from the inside out and God's New Covenant is perfected as we, in obedience, allow his spirit to flow from us, producing the fruit of the Holy Spirit, no longer the rebellious fruit from Adam.

## 11. Jesus

Jesus is the Word made flesh, and he is the one who proceeds from the Father (progenitor), which is the first, the creator of all. But Jesus wasn't created, he was always God and His is the Christ spirit incarnated into a human body.

In the account of the beginning of the human era he was with God and was God and then he made himself lower than divine to reunite heaven and earth although heaven only exists due to that split. John 10:30 quotes Jesus saying, 'The Father and I are one.' (ESV)

Jesus, or Jeshua, as he would have been known while on earth, acted as a self-proclaimed rabbi and his followers called him that, rabbi, teacher, or master.

They knew the Rabbinic code that a rabbi displayed the character of his own teacher and so Jeshua acted out of the character of his father, the creator, the progenitor of all life. That was why he said, 'If you have seen me, you have seen the Father.'

This book cannot begin to do justice to a study of Jesus Christ, so I'll leave that with you for your studies and desire to get to know him better.

173

## 12. Repentance

What's the problem with repentance? Does our earthbound ego sometimes get in the way of our turning from the legacy of rebellion to the call of God in our lives?

In the Bible, repentance, a turning from sin, a turning away from the patterns of the world, a turning towards Jesus, towards the Father reaped blessings and broke the curses imposed at the fall.

A repentance of the mind, soul, spirit, heart, whatever we can repent with, is God's command for us to fall back into adoption, into His family and the inheritance promised to us.

We can enjoy life by clearing up the misunderstanding about the mind and seeing the importance of thought and consciousness as gifts by which to navigate life on earth. Iif we stop there, we are only then still 'of the world' but when we see the nature of the inside-out Kingdom of God, then we have the chance to experience a supernatural heaven-based walk on planet earth just like Jesus. The power to do that comes because we will be 'in Christ' and he in us.

## 13. The New Kingdom

When Jesus roamed the communities of the Middle East, he went to the 'lost sheep of Israel' because he had to introduce the New Covenant in action rather than just words.

The pre-covenants were wordy and based on imposed rules and laws, but they just prepared the way for the Messiah.

Jesus spoke of a Kingdom that was 'not of this world', as he taught both Jewish leaders and Roman citizens, because both groups were demonstrating fruit of the old mind, Jews in their religion and Romans in their brutal domination. Both groups were innocently acting out the me-first mind, so Jesus had to operate in an opposite nature.

## 14. Living Sacrifices, Living Temples—the Indwelling God

Because the old covenants required blood sacrifice through the destruction of substitutionary animals, this sacrificial death was fulfilled once and for all in Christ through the cross, to initiate the New Covenant.

Humans no longer need to do that animal sacrifice, but we have become living sacrifices when we obey him and live in Christ.

Due to this progression in the covenants, there is no longer need for the external temple as the dwelling place of God.

We shouldn't confuse the church buildings with the old holy temples.

The tabernacle was the early dwelling place of God's word, the scriptures. When the word (scripture) became flesh (Christ) the tabernacle moved into the human through the Holy Spirit.

## 15. Beatitudes: How the New Mind Produces Holy Fruit

Jesus showed his new Kingdom in both words and actions. The words of his sermons were fresh and different, no one had heard anything like them, and they seemed, on face value to be in direct conflict with the law of the old covenants.

What Jesus was teaching in his words was the new way of living that would emanate from the regenerated mind. This new mind came from the Kingdom of Heaven, not from the world that was still destined to operate from the unregenerated mind, unless they accepted Jesus as the Messiah.

The actions that Jesus displayed—healings, walking on water, turning water to wine and so on—were demonstrations of the authority his spiritual Kingdom had over the material earth, a supernatural power that humans could not understand or repeat even though many were able to demonstrate earthly versions of the Kingdom through philosophy and magic.

Creation has always been spiritually rooted, the visible manifesting from the invisible. Humans have the inherent ability to perform miracles and preach a different lifestyle without repentance, but the creator God warned of such behaviour throughout the old covenant era and his chosen Kings and leaders lost their blessings, their jobs, and their lives through such rebellion.

Human attempts at enlightening the mind through spiritual practices that are not aligned with scripture still lack trusting in God's prominence in the whole of creation, and even though they might have good intention, calling on earthbound practices can lead to pride, manipulation and control.

## 16. Death—Necessary for New Birth

When Jesus conquered death, the curse from the fall was nullified and the effect of this is that believers who are in Christ will be saved for the renewal of all creation which will be physically manifested from Jesus, who is described as the living 'Word of God'.

We can see that death still currently affects the human flesh during this transitionary period.

We need to be factual about what we are experiencing. It doesn't do us any favours to have blind faith and hope for the best. What we experience is dying flesh, decaying in the environment as the old creation is dying under the effects of the curse, except for those who see the spiritual nature of the transitional human era.

## 17. The Cross—Death to the Old Self

There are cataclysmic events that have shaped and reshaped the human era such as earthquakes, floods, asteroids perhaps wiping out the dinosaurs, space travel, reorganisation of the continents through changing climates, but nothing has or ever will supersede the cross of Jesus's death and his resurrection, ascension, and the entry of the Holy Spirit into the hearts of humans.

The cross of Barabbas (see Matthew 27:15) was waiting for the criminal until the crowd decided that Jesus should be crucified in his place. The cross was a brutal way to die, but even worse was the scourging, the stripping of flesh for the victim chained to a post and whipped with leather thongs made more horrific with glass and bone insets. That Barabbas cross, meant for the rebel, meant for us, was taken by Jesus.

## 18. Resurrection—Risen to New Life

This is where we see the power of the Trinity of God. Although this is a mystery way beyond comprehension of the old mind, The 'father' or 'progenitor' undertakes a cataclysmic shift in the history of the human era.

Jesus shifts from an incarnate human/divine hybrid to become a new creation, one of a far superior nature from the earth and humanity at that time. In the spiritual realm, Jesus had overturned the celestial universal rebellion battle of the pre-human era and conquered death and Hades, which had been active as a result of the fall. He would spend a time phasing between heaven and earth for about forty days when he would 'appear' to many as evidence of his resurrection, before he would return to the Father to enable the release of the Holy Spirt.

## 19. Ascension—the Return to the Father

'Righteousness is available because I go to the Father, and you will see me no more,' (John 16:10, NLT).

'Don't cling to me for I haven't yet ascended to the Father but go find my brothers and tell them "I am ascending to my Father and your Father, to my God and your God,"' (John 20:17, NLT).

We talk a lot about the cross and the resurrection, but I think the ascension is largely misunderstood, especially as it sort of backs up the misunderstanding that heaven is a place in the sky. I'm not writing any additional notes here, I think the words of Jesus justify themselves. Please also read John 16:28. 'Yes, I came from the Father into the world and now I will leave the world and return to the Father,' (NLT).

## 20. Prophecy of the Coming Holy Spirit

During the period when God was speaking through his chosen people, which we call the prophets, the Holy Spirit and the inside-out Kingdom was a future theme, but it was clearly evident that a new, better arrangement was on its way and in Hebrews 10:16 the writer quotes an Old Testament prophet Jeremiah, 'This is the New Covenant I will make with my people on that day, says the Lord, I will put my laws in their hearts and I will write them on their minds.' This sounds like an inside-out promise to me!

In John 16:7, Jesus is quoted as saying 'It is to your advantage that I go away for if I do not go away the helper will not come to you but if I go I will send him to you.

## 21. Holy Spirit

The Holy Spirit has often been misunderstood and for many years I thought of this aspect of God to be the smallest and least able to grasp. If we think of the Holy Spirit as the 'breath of God', it makes a bit more sense to the creation, the fall and then the re-creation story of this human era. However, the Holy Spirit is way more than an aspect or breath of God. The Holy Spirit is God.

In the beginning, the breath, spirit, or Word of God was hovering over the dark chaos of planet earth and then the Father spoke creation of sentient life on the planet. The Lord God made Adam from the soil (a carbon creature) and breathed the spirit into him, and he came alive. When Jesus sent out his disciples, he breathed on them and said, 'Receive the Holy Spirit'. There can't really be any other way of Jesus being resurrected than the Father breathing life into his dead body so that, in turn, having returned to the Father, Jesus could breathe that Holy Spirit into the apostles to give them supernatural power to undertake the mission that he had appointed them to fulfil: 'For you will receive power when the Holy Spirit comes upon you...'

The Holy Spirit, breath, or ghost, as he was called in early Bible translations, is the power and will of the Godhead, the Trinity of three.

The Holy Spirit empowers the new regenerated mind and, just to clarify his identity further, in the book of Acts he is referred to as the 'Spirit of Jesus'. In his letter to the Philippians, Paul writes, 'For I know that as you pray for me, and the Spirit of Jesus Christ helps me, this will lead to my deliverance,' (Philippians 1:19, NLT)

## 22. Acts of the Holy Spirit

After Jesus's resurrection, the disciples seemed to be a bit lost as what to do next. When personal thought is confused or lacks direction, our actions can become sporadic and less co-ordinated.

Some of the disciples went back to their previous default identities as fishermen. Jesus knew that would happen and so he met them on the shore and cooked them breakfast, had a chat and reassured them that the mission was due to enter a new and revolutionary phase, so they should be ready for action.

The subsequent acts of the apostles, as set out in the book of the title in the Bible, are really the acts of the Holy Spirit renewing minds and, as that happened, the belief, faith, and power was realised and the mission expanded—well, actually it exploded throughout the world, around the Mediterranean and beyond.

People are the focus of the book because it is natural for us to focus on the external, the outcomes prove the changes, but the book is really all about how the inside-out revelation was being lived out in the world.

## 23. Apostles as Jews and Gentiles

The book of Acts and the letters from the apostles are clear evidence of the new mind creating new behaviours.

The power to change internally stokes the motivation to change externally. Feelings of security, connection and love grew through faith, and motivated fearless, selfless actions.

The me-first old mind has been set aside to create space for new thinking, different feelings, and radical actions.

This is God's new paradigm and the world will never be the same again.

The Jewish apostles still showed a respectful display of the religious laws and although at times they fall back into regulations such as Sabbath rules and circumcision, the new mind is evident in the attitudes of those who saw the light, that love and acceptance in Christ overrules judgement and classification.

Paul, as the new kid on the apostolic block, takes time to visit Jerusalem and meet with the elders to ensure he would not cause division or offense as he takes the great news of God's grace and love to the non-Jews, the Gentiles.

Despite apparent differences of opinion regarding culture, and the diversity ingrained in their old thinking routines, Paul's mission becomes the focus, to love and serve their Lord in the new era of human development.

## 24. Paul as the Model of New Creation

The uniqueness of Paul, as far as the Bible tells us, was that his calling was directly from the new Jesus in his risen form, directly from the Lord's mouth, a booming voice, a flashing light, sufficient to send this proud Jewish murderer of Christians sprawling, blinded, in the dust of the road to Damascus.

Paul was immediately led to a house in Damascus where he would meet another disciple called Ananias whom God had appeared to in a vision, giving the instruction to visit the house where Paul was staying and pray for him to receive his sight back.

Ananias resisted at first because he was aware of Paul's reputation as the primary persecutor of the new Christian movement but Jesus insisted and so Ananias obeyed.

This encounter resulted in Paul getting more than his sight back, as he also received the Holy Spirit and was commissioned to take the "good news" of Jesus to the non-Jewish communities, known as the Gentiles.

Jesus supernaturally changes Paul from the inside out, installing His spirit, a new mind and a heart of love and compassion and so begins a mission that would the change the history of humanity forever.

Paul's phenomenal writings display that he was an intelligent scholar and a zealot for the Jewish cause. We are immensely blessed to have on record the power of God displayed in the changing of Paul's mind and heart, these are surely the most important accounts on the implications of God's New Covenant and our inside-out revelation.

## 25. In Christ

In the Church we sometimes struggle to 'qualify' people in terms of their Christian status.

This reflection of the old mind still at work in the Church potentially creates division and judgement between those who are 'just churchgoers', 'ordinary believers', 'born-again believers', and just plain old 'Christians'. So what does Paul say about this in terms of his vision for the Church? Is Paul's writing still relevant in our non-inclusive society that pretends to be inclusive but is more divisive than ever?

Paul uses the term 'in Christ' throughout his letters and I want to suggest that this description is a clean and tidy way to bring us all into the body of believers, in a way that Paul intended.

The body of Christ, the Church, is all inclusive in terms of the spirit, not behaviour. If we judge each other by what we do rather than who we are 'in Christ', we start up a hierarchy and that is open to misuse.

Study Paul's letters for yourself and see what you think of the description in Christ. See if there are any references to being in Christ in the other letters attributed to the early apostles (see 1 Peter:5).

## 26. Church

I'm going to bring us back to 'church' as was probably the original term for the community of people who are in Christ. This is because, if the regenerated mind is what helps us to realise the new life, we have the amazing opportunity to live differently, and then all of us in the community will realise that at any given time we are in varying stages of living out that regeneration and we all help each other in that unfolding revelation.

If the church is just the place where we go on Sundays to sing songs and listen to sermons, then we are in danger of that place becoming the dwelling place of God rather than in ourselves. If we 'go to church', then a separation arises that God is outside in and that is not the case.

A quick look at the book of Acts and we will see that the believers met sometimes in the temple and sometimes in people's homes. It's not so much where we meet, but that we do meet, and when we meet, we encourage each other to grow in the new mind and consequently the renewed heart.

## 27. The Story Continues—Acting Out of the New Mind

One of the most inspiring passages in the book of Acts, for me, is the final one.

After years of mission, surviving prison, shipwrecks, snakebites, and floggings, this happens:

'Paul lived two more years in Rome in his own rented quarters, welcoming all who came to visit. He continued to proclaim to all the truths of God's Kingdom realm, teaching them about the Lord Jesus, the Anointed One, speaking triumphantly and without any restriction,' (Acts 28:30–31, TPT).

There have been two hundred decades since then. If a generation is twenty-five years, that means something like eighty generations have passed and still humanity tries to blow itself off the face of its home planet.

The hope is that in every generation, millions of people are hearing the gospel Paul loved so much. Some respond, some don't, and that's God's gift to us of free will in action. It's also the parable of the sower in action, that parable that Jesus taught all those years earlier (Luke 8:4–11, Matthew 13:18, Mark 4:13).

## 28. The Principles of the Mind

Did Paul understand the principles of the mind as we do now?

That's not specifically given space in scripture, and maybe Paul would have argued that they were some form of Greek philosophy, but in fairness there have been many different ideas and theories during the intervening generations.

He wrote to the Corinthian Church in 1 Corinthians Chapter 2, 'And I, when I came to you, brothers, I did not come proclaiming to you the testimony of God with lofty speech or wisdom,' (ESV). In verse 5 he continues, '… so that your faith might not rest on human wisdom but on God's power,' (NIV).

Paul's teaching was lost to the world for decades as the scriptures were locked in Latin tomes for years, and then there were the dark ages. In fact, we do well to jump those intervening eras and tie the teaching from two thousand years ago as described in the Bible to today's cultures. We need not concern ourselves with acts that took place in the darker times because they were still driven by the rebellious mind and really, is life that different now?

Desert communities still exist as they did then, and in many parts of the populated world tribal life still thrives.

So, we can look at the benefits that the principles bring to our understanding of the human operating system in any culture, because they exist before form. We can see that all humans, irrespective of culture and education, use the principles to operate the old mind or the new mind, the main difference being that the Bible teaches that the truly renewed mind is entwined with the Holy Spirit when we are in Christ.

Because the principles are fundamental to the way humans experience life on earth, we can conclude that they have always been operating, and Paul preached in power, not words.

Our spirituality under the new renewed mind should easily accept power and not words as the indication of change.

Syd Banks asked us not to listen to his words but feel the feeling beyond the words. He knew something about the mind of God, and I am grateful for his uncovering of the principles because knowing this releases us from the legacy of humanistic psychology, but Syd's principles do not go as far as the fundamentals of biblical teaching about sin, the cross, redemption, and adoption into the family of the creator.

## 29. Devil, Deception and Distraction

The 'three Ds' that keep people trapped within a veil of confusion.

Satan in his guise of the Devil has become an object of jokes, Halloween masks, and dodgy horror movies, so should we ignore all that devil talk because it's not real, just a distraction from proper life?

As we've seen so far, according to the Bible, Lucifer was involved with God before the human era and continues to spread deception throughout humanity with his schemes.

Some might say that he operates very close to the truth, just providing enough of the truth to deceive us into error. The regenerated mind, powered by the Holy Spirit, which Jesus called the advocate, the counsellor, is the weapon God has provided for us to shield ourselves from Lucifer's wiles.

In his letter to the Ephesians, Paul writes about us putting on the armour of God 'to protect us from the Devil's schemes' so I don't think I'm far off in my guidance for us to work on this internally, guard our hearts and minds, meditate on scripture as we experience the event cycle, see where we might be hearing misguided thinking and realign and recalibrate to the Holy Spirit.

## 30. The New Mind in Christ

Read 1 Corinthians 2:6 until the end of that chapter. This letter by Paul sets out beautifully the mind of Christ (the Holy Spirit, wisdom) and the mind of the world (intellectual, habitual wisdom of the collective human spirit).

Paul sums this all up with the statement 'but we have the mind of Christ,' (1 Corinthians 2:16, ESV).

Here's the similarity but also the difference between the principles enlightened view of life and the biblical way of life, and I stress that there is a difference:

Principles: Our practice is to acknowledge that our personal mind is in a constant state of flux. Thoughts come and go and the feelings they produce make our experience seem so real, and if we are caught up in our own personal mind, we may experience a 'reality' that is tainted by our past, tainted by our habits, and tainted by our projections. Universal divine mind is the energy of all things, if we 'drop out' of our personal thinking we will find peace and contentment in universal mind because it is divine energy, the source of all things. In this divine energy, we find the wisdom we need from moment to moment to live a fully engaged life based on love and understanding each other with creativity and unlimited access to universal resources.

Bible: Our practice is to repent from the activities we produce from the thoughts and feelings arising from the Satanic mind of rebellion against God, which produce fear, insecurity, judgement, competition, and criticism. This old mind drives our behaviour and because external laws do not have the power to change us, the change must come from the inside out. God's Holy Spirit is part of the trinitarian Godhead, the creator and sustainer of all life on earth, and God the Holy Spirit provides inside-out power and guidance to live a life demonstrated by Jesus when he was on earth, of love and understanding. In ourselves we do not possess the power to change our behaviour and so God does this from the inside out through his own spirit working with ours. So, we must ignore the 'old mind with its worldly patterns' and 'put on the new mind', from which the fruit of God the Holy Spirit will flow.

Further into Paul's first letter to the Corinthians he describes the fruit of the Holy Spirit, which is the character and nature of God himself:

'Love is patient, love is kind. It does not envy, it does not boast, it is not proud. It does not dishonour others, it is not self-seeking, it is not easily angered, it keeps no record of wrongs. Love does not delight in evil but rejoices with the truth. It always protects, always trusts, always hopes, always perseveres,' 1 Corinthians 13:4–8 (ESV).

The Holy Spirit is God's gift to us. He IS the mind of Christ, in fact He is the Spirit of Jesus (Acts 16:6) and he is called the promise of our inheritance in the Kingdom of God, the invisible inside-out Kingdom that manifests through us into the lost and broken world.

## 31. Forgiveness

There is a spiritual principle throughout the Bible which states that we must forgive others as God has in Jesus has forgiven us. I appreciate this principle is more apparent in the New Testament, but as Jesus is the self-proclaimed 'fulfilment of the Law' then it must logically also be inherent in God's earlier covenants with humanity.

In his letter to the Colossian church, the Apostle Paul writes "Make allowance for each other's faults, and forgive anyone who offends you. Remember, the Lord forgave you, so you must forgive others." (Colossians 3:13, NLT).

Jesus himself had taught his followers the importance of forgiving others, as illustrated in Luke's writings, "Do not judge, and you will not be judged. Do not condemn, and you will not be condemned. Forgive, and you will be forgiven." (Luke 6:37, NIV), and famously, from the cross, among his last words, Jesus cried out, "Father. forgive them for they don't know what they are doing." (Luke 23:34, NLT).

# Chapter Eleven

# Alternative Spirituality

*'You cannot travel on the path unless you become the path itself.'*
*Buddha.*

## Introduction

*Although I decided in 1988 to believe the Bible and accept God's offer of Jesus as my saviour, I found that temptations to still explore deeper things of God beyond the Bible was always in my mind. It wasn't that I was still unsatisfied, but there are always those questions of 'what if' going on in the background, so I won't pretend it's been easy sailing.*

*When my first marriage ended, I found that the church I had been attending was a difficult place for a single, divorced man. I met and married a new love partner who wasn't a Christian and who practised occult, and it wasn't long before I put my Bible-based beliefs on the shelf and fell into her world of humanistic spirituality, starting to practice more self-development. Soon I was teaching humanistic self-improvement and universal spirituality as a 'guru'.*

*When I fell back in line with God, I still wanted to help all seekers of freedom from the patterns of the world, and so I'm not excluding alternative spirituality and, in fact, I believe this can still be a route to enlightenment. It is followed by millions all over the world and I believe that the Holy Spirit can and will guide those in search of truth.*

*I'm not talking about alternative religions here. I'm only interested in spiritual alternatives to the Bible teaching.*

## The Principles as a Spiritual Model

The principles of mind consciousness and thought are nothing new in the sense that they are the fundamental building blocks of our psychological experience, and have always existed.

Just as Everest was the still the tallest mountain before humans discovered it, mind, consciousness, and thought have always been our operating system's components., We didn't 'see' how they worked together in the way they do until Sydney Banks had his enlightenment experience in 1973.

The concept of a spiritual realm, where there is peace from our human troubles, has been the subject of exposition and exploration for as long as we have been able to write things down, and probably before that.

The fundamental insecurity and fear embedded in the human condition cannot be explained without the foundation stories in the Bible and other ancient writings but all of this conjecture has led to a fundamental problem of duality: the problem of 'there' being better than 'here' or there being more peaceful than here, and those ideas, in our modern society and culture, manifest as a fear of missing out. 'I'll be happy when I'm there' suggests that I am unhappy here!

Duality says that there is a spirit world and a physical world.

Spiritual psychotherapies such as mindfulness seek to focus more time on the present, so this is not escapism. Meditation encompasses the whole human experience, recognising that our physical experience manifests from our spiritual source.

If you read or listen to Sydney Banks, Eckhart Tolle, or Allan Watts, the messages are similar: In this present moment the ocean is calm but when we think about the past or the future, we become the surface waves of circumstance and that's when we get into trouble.

## Is the Bible Relevant?

Maybe it's because of the Bible's reputation of being old and stuffy that it's not easily recognised as a spiritual guide to enlightenment. Even when I was first fully engaged in the Church, I read alternative writings that were outside of the recognised canon of scripture.

There are many writings beyond the Bible that can raise our historical and spiritual awareness and there is a wealth of history in, say, the book of Enoch or the Gospel of Thomas, but those who decided what was in or out of the Bible left them out,

The Bible in my opinion doesn't need updating by new interpretations in books and movies such as *The Secret* or *A Course in Miracles*, promoted as updated bulletins from the spiritual newsdesk of Jesus or Abraham Hicks.

Jesus said from the cross, 'It is finished,' and the New Testament warns not to add to what has already been laid down in Revelation as the end of the present human age and the creation of the new one.

Like Jesus himself, I'm not interested in religions. Once humans get hold of an idea and make out it comes from God, we're on sticky ground.

However, having spent time exploring all of the occult practices I feel qualified to include them in this book of the mind, because my experience was that the further I travelled from the Holy Spirit, the nearer I came to a dark and lonely death, both spiritually and physically, and I took other innocent people along for the ride.

## 'Not Religious, But Spiritual'

Religion is outside in. Where humans make rules about spiritual laws, they are grounding those laws in the old operating system.

In order to escape from the illusion of duality, alternative spirituality becomes very close to the practice known as Gnosticism, that was around just after Jesus's time on earth.

The Gnostics thought they had a deeper understanding of the spiritual nature of human life, claiming that Jesus was probably a manifestation of a spirit that showed up from time to time, a sort of Gaia. They were 'chosen' as spiritual mentors and guides.

This teaching is that humanity is evolved through such spirit beings coming onto the scene to teach us mortals enlightenment.

## Self-focused Psychology

The search for 'self' probably goes back to the dawn of the human age when we were cast out of the garden and destined to scratch out a living in the wilderness. We have been searching for Eden, but God has spiritually closed the gates unless we ask Jesus to let us back in.

In generational innocence, detached from the origin event of rebellion, our early ancestors would have just taken it at face value that human life was a battle, a struggle—life and death in the wilderness.

At some stage, not only were God's chosen people such as Moses, Abraham, and David aware of there being a different way of life, but Satan surely wouldn't have sat back and watched God make his move without bringing his own distraction to the party.

## The Search for God or the Search for Self?

The search for God creates religions. If we try to reach a God in the sky, we end up projecting ourselves up there.

Recently it has been discovered that there is a part in the brain that is like a higher power, a state of super-consciousness or meta-consciousness which can serve as our 'god' because it is literally and metaphorically 'higher' than both our executive and reptile brains.

The meta-conscious is 'over all' other brain activities but it's still programmed by our thoughts and lived experience and so is still part of us, albeit seemingly more intelligent and tuned into a spiritual wavelength.

This might be because it produces thoughts that are not easily recognised as habitual but more inspired, such as when we get new ideas when in the shower, walking the dog, or driving the car.

This gives us hope of evolution to a better way of thinking that might save humanity, but that's not God's plan, which is a new creation, not a renovation job on the old one.

## Finding Self

What do we find when we find ourselves?

We find ourselves!

When introducing spirituality into intake conversations with new clients, I always ask, 'Do you think there is more to life?' or 'Do you spin this planet and order the seasons?' although I need to be careful to whom I ask such questions because, strangely, people can take offence at such a deep and personal level of enquiry. These offences are echoes of the shame that Adam and Eve showed in the garden when they realised they were naked before God.

The root of the me-first mind is insecurity so it will naturally be looking for some form of 'home' and so, when we are unable to find that in the material world, we look at alternatives.

That search elsewhere raises the question of creation or evolution and that can either take us beyond ourselves to another being or we close the loop and suggest that, when we find the creator, it will have been ourselves all along.

It seems illogical to deny the existence of a higher power when it's obvious that no human that has ever existed could create a gnat, let alone a universe.

What, then, is the point of self-first spirituality?

It might be that, because we are fundamentally unhappy and insecure, when we have completed our search for those qualities in a material world occupied by people with the same problem, we think we need to search further afield.

If the answer isn't out there on the horizontal plane, maybe it's up a few levels?

So we get on board the elevator and press the up button (because we don't want to go down to hell, do we?) and we begin to detach from the material world of disappointment in the search for that higher meaning.

## Enlightenment Spirituality

Is there still such a thing as New Age or is this just old habits repeating?

Popular from the 1970s until around the turn of this century, New Age is probably in its final stages as the world seeks different experiences, those which might be more acceptable to the mainstream and to business and certainly less woo-woo, which doesn't seem so acceptable anymore.

Mindfulness and principles of energy and manifestation are easily sold now in business development. Putting a technical slant on spirituality made it easier for me to sell mindfulness to car design engineers and the event cycle was very well received by designers.

With their 'power from beyond' weekends wrapped up in such a way as to give their company the edge over the competition, business coaches can still get away with wearing beads as long as they are genuinely from Camden Market.

From the point of view of this book, New Age spirituality is a me-first, ego-based activity which is part of the search for truth in terms of a viable alternative to Bible-based spiritual teaching.

There has been a focus on external objects as having some sort of power or influence. Crystals, icons, bracelets, amulets, and so forth carry energetic powers and different types of stones and rocks have healing or alternative powers.

New Age is a real catch-all and was a powerful anti-religion to the Church during the eighties when a lot of pop music and art cultures were influenced by New Age energy and teachings.

The latest iteration of New Age can be seen in the various enlightenment spiritualities.

Paul, in his New Testament letters warned of alternative teachings. One test of someone being a Christian was whether they accepted that Jesus had come in the flesh rather than being an enlightened or spirit being. The apostle John wrote this warning:

'This is how you can recognise the spirit of God: every spirit that acknowledges that Jesus Christ has come in the flesh is from God but every spirit that does not acknowledge Jesus is not from God,' (1 John 4:2–3, NIV).

I can speak with some authority about New Age spirituality, having spent ten years in that zone, going deeper and deeper into a loveless void.

Even the spiritual practices from other cultures never fitted like a glove and the community was often very competitive and could be judgemental at times.

New Age and alternative spirituality can often be shown to be no more than a projection of ourselves in the ultimate deception that there is a greater self with whom we can trust but to be real about it, we often can't trust our little selves, let alone a bigger self somewhere out in the ether.

### Me-First Mind vs You-First Mind

1 Corinthians 13 is sometimes called the love chapter. In it, Paul describes what love is according to the Kingdom of God, and it's the opposite of the me-first emphasis of the world's system.

The old mind is me first, the new mind is you first, or God first, and the fruit of such teachings is the proof and evidence of their roots and sources.

## The Universe as God

The universe is a popular god in the world, an acceptable spiritual source of data, influence, and provision beyond us.

Some say we are the universe and others separate themselves from it so that it can provide for them.

At the end of the day, it's identity, love, and purpose that we are all seeking as the direct result of our first ancestors giving those things up.

To set up viable alternatives to God the creator, Satan comes up with what seems to be acceptable, attractive, and stimulating ways to maintain and stimulate to the old me-first mind.

The universe might be attributed sometimes to have come up with a new job, partner, or bright red Porsche, but what it can't provide is love, unconditional acceptance, peace, and contentment.

That is what's lacking in the concept of the universe as a god.

The universe is made from intelligent energy, and you can try to love it, but can it love you?

## How Does the Universe Become God?

Culturally, the Bible, God, and Jesus is often a mockery and a joke because, when we are busy gaining a godless education, working in a godless job, and surrounded by death, disease, and destruction, some distant careless deity is of little relevance or value.

There is no need for a historic god if things are going ok for us and we're busily ignoring our insecurities through our busy jobs, relationships and gathering possessions, building our little personal Edens.

There might, however, come a time when we could do with a bit of help and that's when the universe can become an option to give us a leg up, get us a bit closer to that better life, relationship, or house in the woods or by the ocean.

The great thing about the universe as god is that we don't need to change, or repent, or give up booze for Lent. In fact, the universe seems remarkably like a super-version of ourselves. It seems to want what we want and if we believe and keep our focus, super algorithms of the creative universe will manifest our desires.

The universe becomes the ultimate inside-out projection of our greatest desires.

What can possibly go wrong?

The universe can be your best friend and your worst enemy.

In my life, for a time, I had forsaken the God of the Bible for the universe as god and it was a very dark and lonely experience.

## Loss of Love

The great sense of loss that many people suffer when they fall out of a family or love relationship haunts us and overshadows our efforts to focus on building a new life.

Finding ourselves in a shared house with others suffering through the same core loss is not in itself enough to create an environment for sustained change. We need to know about the love, acceptance, and unconditional love that is described in the Bible and that becomes real when practised, but it's often perceived as more hard work.

If we see restoring a relationship with God through Jesus as a type of 'religious' relationship that takes effort when we are already tired and unsure of ourselves, then the thought of a benevolent universal power that doesn't hold any grudges can seem like a real alternative to the stuffy old God of the Bible.

The attraction is that the universe can be anything we want it to be and one of the dangers is that flexibility of interpretation can include a projection of our doubts and insecurities from our wounded psyche.

There must be an external framework to support the internal changes.

This is a cultural issue resulting from our educational system, fractured families, and high-pressure working environment; all these are contaminated with conditions, challenges, suspicion, hidden agendas but the Kingdom of God is completely different, God does it all.

The fact is that God has done it all for us: Read 1 Peter 1:18 and other scriptures about God's covenants. God always takes the initiative; all we need to do is be grateful and accept it all.

So an impersonal universal energy is a decent explanation for the spiritual structure of the created universe but it's insufficient as the personal unconditional lover of all creation, who works tirelessly 24/7 to make redemption a living experience in these times.

**God as Our Redemption is Not a Spiritual Escape Hatch**

As a caring people, how do we bring an unconditional feeling of love to those who have experienced pain and disappointment, and who often live in regret that the life they now have to live is punishment for failing to control feelings, actions, behaviour, anger, habits, and addictions?

External activity is always conditional, even if unconsciously so, because we all live in separate, filtered realities: if I don't match your expectations or you don't match mine, that makes it all conditional.

Jesus's teaching and Paul's advice to churches can be interpreted both as conditional, because they ask us to behave a certain way, and unconditional because of the grace of God who provides us with the power to live this new life.

Churches extrapolate the conditionality and so often people feel judged if they fail in the material life.

The lure of the universe as god is that the testimonies we hear are almost always positive. I wanted a partner and the universe provided. I wanted a new car and the universe provided. I really wanted that new job, and the universe came up trumps. We rarely hear that the universe has failed, and where do we go if that happens?

If the universe hasn't come up trumps it's because it's still working on it or because I'm still waiting, still chanting, still affirming and the problem isn't me, it's just my patience that is being tested.

In our innocence we've also attributed these universal excuses to God-out-there as well.

When the impersonal, vacuous energy of the universe isn't enough we will give it a personality and call it God. That leads us even further into deception if that God is not the one shown by Jesus and powered by the Spirit and scriptural teaching.

To find the source of unconditional love, we must fall into the space beyond and before the created universe into the heart of God, the creator.

# Chapter Twelve

# The Principles in Scripture

*'The Kingdom is not discovered in one place or another, for God's Kingdom realm is already expanding within some of you,'* Luke 17:21 (TPT).

## Introduction

*As I returned from the world of crystals, Tarot, animism, and dualism to my first love, the God of the Bible, I needed to reassure myself that I was back on track and my big question professionally was whether I should still be teaching Three Principles and the inside-out psychology, or was this an open door that needed closing to me?*

*I needed to see how that psychology fitted in with the Bible message of how life and the mind works.*

*This chapter looks at how the principles of mind, consciousness and thought are described in the Bible and in Jesus's teaching of the inside-out Kingdom of Heaven.*

*The theme of this part of the book is about being mindful of conceding to the renewed mind. Surrendering every moment of our life to the sufficient care found in the mind of God. Admitting that the presence of God is true, proper, and certain. It is sufficient.*

## Authority

'Jesus came to them and said, "All authority in heaven and earth has been given to me,"' (Matthew 28:18, ESV).

For many people God is an impersonal universal energy, but the Bible tells of a God of love determined to reconcile his creation to himself and when Jesus stated that all authority had been given to him, that means that ultimately all paths to life lead to him as the gatekeeper of the spiritual realm.

We all have a choice to believe or not but when Jesus made his claim, he was either telling the truth or spinning a lie and if he was lying then he must have been one of the most egotistical creatures to ever walk planet earth.

### Divine Mind or the Mind of Christ?

Maybe we don't think we use the term divine enough in the mainstream Church. I thought the term divine was a bit loose when Syd Banks referred to 'divine mind consciousness and thought'. In an early teaching Syd spoke of Christ consciousness as a 'super-conscious state' so my issue is can divine, in the way Syd had experienced it, refer to the Father, Son and Spirit of the Bible, or is it some otherness?

Why don't we use the term *divine* much in Church to describe God?

Is it too New Age? Maybe we need to claim New Age back for the Kingdom of Jesus?

The mind of Christ *is* divine mind. So, does that give Christ consciousness personality?

Jesus was always the Spirit but took on the nature of man when he came to earth to be a sacrifice for sin, and to defeat the Devil, who is a captive spiritually

When he ascended to the Father, he sent the Holy Spirit to be our helper, guide, and advocate—these are qualities Syd attributed to divine wisdom.

I'm questioning, is Syd's divine wisdom the mind of Christ?

## Peace of Mind or the Mind of Christ?

So ,when I concede my personal, programmed, tainted, confused, and overthinking mind to the mind of Christ, do I get the peace and wisdom I get when I concede to the mind of the divine God of the principles?

Are we looking for peace of mind or the mind of Christ?

Jesus said, 'Peace I leave with you, my peace I give to you. Not as the world gives do I give to you,' (John 14:27, ESV).

Has our focus on the earthly Jesus spoiled our mystic relationship with the divine? Have we become too limited and grounded?

Jesus gave the gift of peace to his followers, his disciples, who were not born again, and so we must see that once the Holy Spirit came, God's spirit is within us, not out in the universe somewhere. We are turning out more like the model of translated humanity demonstrated by Paul.

What is the most up-to-date description of Jesus in the Bible? Have a look at how he shows up in the book of Revelation!

## Psycho–Spiritual Principles

I brought the principles into my practice as my main operational paradigm in 2013.

For ten years I have seen wonderful changes in my clients, Christian and not Christian, but I always had a nagging feeling in the back of my mind that something was missing.

So let's explore further if and how and where the principles of mind, consciousness, and thought appear in scripture.

Is it an undeniable fact that God and His creation have a heart, a mind, and thoughts?

Let's have a look.

## Principles of Mind in the Old Testament (First Covenants)

Psalm 92:5 'How great are your works, Lord, how profound your thoughts (NIV).

Psalm 139:2 'You know when I sit and when I rise; you perceive my thoughts from afar,' (NIV).

Isaiah 26:3 'You will keep him in perfect peace, whose minds are steadfast because they trust in you,' (NIV).

Isaiah 55:8 'For my thoughts are not your thoughts neither are your ways my ways, says the Lord,' (NIV).

Daniel 7:15 'I, Daniel, was troubled in spirit and the visions that passed through my mind disturbed me,' (NIV).

Deuteronomy 11:18 'Fix these words of mine in your hearts and minds,' (NIV).

Ecclesiastes 1:12–13 'I, the Teacher, was King over Israel in Jerusalem. I applied my mind to study and explore by wisdom all that is done under the heavens.'

Ecclesiastes 2:3 'I tried cheering myself with wine and embracing folly—my mind still guiding me with wisdom,' (NIV).

Isaiah 65:17 'See I will create new heavens and a new earth. The former things will not be remembered, nor will they come to mind,' (NIV).

Jeremiah 11:20 'But you, Lord Almighty, who judge righteously, and test the heart and mind, let me see your vengeance on them, for to you I have committed my cause.'

Jeremiah 17:10 'I the Lord search the heart and examine mind, to reward each person according to their conduct,' (NIV).

Jeremiah 20:12 'Lord Almighty, you who examine the righteous and probe the heart and mind…' (NIV).

Jeremiah 31:33 'This is the covenant that I will make with the people of Israel, after that time, declares the Lord, I will put my law in their minds and write it on their hearts. I will be their God and they will be my people,' (NIV).

Ezekiel 38:10 'This is what the sovereign Lord says, on that day thoughts will come into your mind, and you will devise an evil scheme,' (NIV).

Numbers 23:19 'God is not human being that he should lie, not a human being that he should change his mind,' (NIV).

1 Samuel 2:35 'I will raise up for myself a faithful priest, who will do according to what is in my heart and in my mind,' (NIV).

Jeremiah 23:16 'This is what the Lord Almighty says: "Do not listen to what the prophets are prophesying to you; they fill you with false hopes, they speak visions from their own minds not from the mouth of the Lord,"' (NIV).

Daniel 2:29 'As your majesty was lying there, your mind turned to things to come, and the revealer of mysteries showed you what was going to happen,' (NIV)

1 Chronicles 28:9 'And you, my son Solomon, acknowledge the God of your father, and serve him with wholehearted devotion and with a willing mind, for the Lord searches every heart and understands every desire and every thought,' (NIV).

Proverbs 1:23 'Repent at my rebuke! Then I will pour out my thoughts to you, I will make known to you my teaching,' (NIV).

Proverbs 15:26 'The Lord detests the thoughts of the wicked…' (NIV).

Micah 4:12 'But they do not know the thoughts of the Lord; they do not understand his plan,' (NIV).

Remember that these promises were from the Lord to the community of believers in the early days of his agreement to save them. They did not have the indwelling Holy Spirit, so they had to live by the promise rather than the fact; faith was key.

If we now turn to one of the New Testament letters by Paul, we read about what God has done for us and how by faith we have the new life now.

## A View of the Renewed Life from Paul's Letter to the Colossian Community

In The Passion Translation (TPT) I found that the way Paul warns of false teaching is described quite clearly and this reminds me of the fear and suspicion I find in the Church about so-called New Age teaching.

I think there will always be false teaching, it's got to be one of Satan's strategies. So, I've done a bit of a deep dive into this letter and picked out some specific references. (I'm not going to do all the work here, why don't you have a go through Paul's other letters seeking out this theme of correct teaching?)

I'm of the opinion that whatever Paul's primary message is in one letter, should follow through to his others, the main differences being the audience he is writing to in terms of their spiritual growth and status in the community they serve.

Paul illustrates some supernatural truths, all God's work, God taking the initiative as it's his covenant with us to complete these acts of redemption and translation to his Kingdom.

We read about terms such as 'treasures' (1:5), 'hearts changed' (1:6), 'empowerment by the Holy Spirit' (1:8), 'reservoirs of every kind of wisdom and spiritual knowledge' (1:9), 'energised with all his explosive power' (1:11), 'rescued us... translated us into the Kingdom' (1:13), 'living in the shadow of your evil thoughts and actions, he reconnected you back to yourself and he released his supernatural power to you' (1:21/2), 'living within you is the Christ' (1:27), and many more throughout the letter.

Regarding human wisdom as opposed to God's wisdom, in 2:8, we have this: 'Beware that no one distracts you or intimidates you in their attempts to lead you astray from Christ's fullness by pretending to be full of wisdom when they're filled with endless arguments of human logic.'

In 2:20, 'For you were included in the death of Christ and have died with him to the religious system and the powers of this world.'

Paul adds to this in the first verse of Chapter 3, 'His resurrection is ours too!' and in verse 5 emphasises our gift of life and power in Christ, 'consider your life in this natural realm as already dead and buried.' and in verse 9, 'Now that you have embraced new creation life as true reality lay aside your old Adam-life with its masquerade and disguise.'

Be encouraged to read and meditate on this teaching and you might find all that the New Age and universal wisdom purports to offer us is very different and weak compared to what is offered in the new life Jesus promises.

## Living With the Renewed Mind

Here is some more Bible teaching suggesting that there are principles to living with a renewed mind.

Firstly, from the New Testament letters to the Churches and Church leaders:

Paul's letter to Timothy (2 Tim 1:7) he writes, 'For God gave us a spirit not of fear, but of power and of love and self-control (or a sound mind),' (ESV).

In Paul's letter to the Church in Rome, often referred to as a masterpiece in Christian literature, the verse which started this entire project for me is 'Do not be conformed to this world but be transformed by the renewal of your mind,' (12:2, ESV).

When writing to the Philippian Church, Paul writes that his behaviour has changed now that he is operating with a mind that is being renewed but he has to play his part in the renewing process, '... but one thing I do, forgetting what lies behind and straining forward to what lies ahead, I press toward the goal for the prize of the upward call of God in Christ Jesus. Let those of us who are mature think this way,' (Philippians 3:13–15, ESV).

Paul also writes in his first letter to the Corinthian Christians, 'For who knows a person's thoughts except the spirit of that person which is in him? So also no one comprehends the thoughts of God except the spirit of God,' (1 Corinthians 2:11, ESV) and in the same chapter, 'For who has understood the mind of the Lord so as to instruct him, but we have the mind of Christ,' (1 Corinthians 2:16, ESV).

If we explore this passage in Corinthians further, we can begin to see the similarity between the psycho–spiritual 'consciousness as observer' and Paul's teaching on the spirit as observer.

This is a key to the inside-out revelation because, if this is true, then that part of our operating system that 'knows a person's thoughts' is nothing less than the human spirit of that person, which is in him. By implication, 'conscious awareness' IS the human's individual spirit, nothing more or less.

So, in fact, mind is spirit (the gift of observing) and thought (the gift of creativity).

When Paul states that no one comprehends the thoughts of God except the spirit of God, that reflects how humans are made in God's image, little gods if you will, with the power to be aware (spirit) and the power to create (thought).

We will dive deeper into this in the next chapter, but it would appear to me, if I take this teaching as true, that the 'observing self' is a just theoretical concept for 'awareness' which replaces the spirit.

In cultural terms, the Hebrew spiritual tradition would accept spirit or 'breath' and wouldn't have an issue with attributing that with the personality of God, whereas the Greek cultural mindset would impersonalise it, make it universal and call it energy or 'universe'.

Here we might have found the fundamental difference between the two routes to enlightenment—one searches for the truth in consciousness, the other finds the truth in the spirit.

To quote Paul again, 'Now we have received not the spirit of the world but the spirit who is from God, that we might understand the things freely given to us by God, and we might impart this in words not taught by human wisdom but taught by the spirit, interpreting spiritual thoughts to those who are spiritual,' (1 Corinthians 2:12, ESV).

211

## Feelings or Faith?

There is so much positivity in Paul's letters but also at times there is struggle and testing, but never doubt. Doubt is part of the old mindset, flowing from the fear and insecurity of our disconnection with God.

But all of the New Testament is God taking the initiative to save us, to adopt us and to love us in Jesus unconditionally.

So, in the psychological model as illustrated by the event cycle, thought creates feelings which in turn are usually the motivator to actions.

However, in the new Kingdom of God, feelings are replaced by faith in God's Word as empowered by His Holy Spirit.

The letter titled Hebrews includes a chapter on faith (Hebrews Chapter 11), which I hope will be useful for this study. In verse 3 we can read, 'By faith we understand that the entire universe was formed at God's command, that what we now see did not come from anything that can be seen,' (Hebrews 11:3, NLT).

We can't get more universal than this, can we? The universe as God takes on a different meaning when we read that the universe was created by God in the first place.

Maybe The Passion Translation gives it a different illustration: 'Faith empowers us to see that the universe was created and beautifully co-ordinated by the power of God's words! He spoke and the invisible realm gave birth to all that is seen,' (TPT).

This is a foundational precept in the Three Principles understanding—that what is visible (form) is created and sustained by what is invisible (formless).

Further study of the writings of such scientists as David Bohm adds technique to the visible/invisible mystery. He is attributed as saying that 'Thought creates the universe and then says it doesn't do it.'

## Jesus Teaching the Inside-Out Kingdom

Initially, I have to say that on re-reading Jesus's teaching in what is called the Beatitudes, or, as I recall one corny old American preacher once calling them, the Beautiful Attitudes, I found the entire teaching to be inside out. In other words, the change we are seeking for a renewing of the mind comes within, from where the Kingdom of Heaven is operating and that is where mind is and that is where God has decided to communicate with us through His Holy Spirit.

This section of the Bible's account of Jesus's direct preaching to the people at the time is also referred to as the Sermon on the Mount. Jesus reflects Jewish Rabbinical tradition by addressing the crowds from a high seat of teaching.

Matthew's Gospel, 5:48, will get us off to a decent start: 'Since you are children of a perfect father in heaven, become perfect like him,' (TPT).

There's a very well-read and much-quoted verse, quoting Jesus, after he's been talking about people worries, fears, and cares of worldly things: 'Seek the Kingdom of God above all else and live righteously and he will give you everything you need, (Matthew 6:24, NLT).

This has been the basis of a lot of teaching about us getting new cars, houses, and love partners but notice it is conditional upon seeking the Kingdom of God first.

Jesus makes one of the most powerful declarations in Matthew 28:18. 'All authority in heaven and on earth has been given to me...' (NIV). That's one to ponder on when the Three Principles stresses the importance of seeking divine wisdom rather than relying on our own personal mind. Jesus has all authority, so seeking his wisdom will take us to the truth.

The Book of Matthew has a lot of Jesus teaching, addressed as it is to a Jewish audience and therefore the Messiah's emphasis on the new inside-out version of the law, fulfilled in himself.

In the other Gospels, we can find more references to the inside-out Kingdom.

In John Chapter 15 from the first verse, Jesus teaches about the supernatural connection we have with God through Him, what he metaphorically refers to as 'The Vine.' 'No branch can bear fruit by itself, it must remain in the vine, neither can you bear fruit unless you remain in me.' That is a wonderful invitation, and, in this passage, Jesus calls the Father the vinedresser!

In John Chapter 6, Jesus refers to the Holy Spirit as the Spirit of truth that won't act independently but only as the Father directs. Again, this declares the one-ness of God and His people.

A final word on God's relationship with us, of trust, and of faith is in Mark's Gospel, stating Jesus's teaching on prayer, in 11:24: '... therefore I tell you, whatever you ask for in prayer, believe that you have received it, and it will be yours,' (NIV).

At this point, we should remember to read scripture verses in the context they were written.

Read a few verses before and after, preferably at least the whole chapter because this verse, out of context, is the invitation to question God when the new, red Ferrari you need for your missionary travels still hasn't materialised on the front drive.

## Creation, Genesis—Form Out of the Formless

Right at the start, in the creation account of Genesis 1: 'In the beginning God created the heavens and the earth. Now the earth was formless and empty, darkness was over the surface of the deep and the spirit of God was hovering over the waters,' (Genesis 1:1, NIV).

In verse 27, 'So God created mankind in his own image, in the image of God he created them, male and female he created them,' although in Genesis 2 there is a different account of God initially creating the man, Adam, before taking a rib from him and making woman as his companion.

The main thing is that God is the original creator, the progenitor. In other words, the Father.

That was then, and now, in God's image we use our mind to think of ideas to which the spirit gives life and brings into being.

## Some Scriptural Principles

Romans 12:2 'Stop imitating the ideals and opinions of the culture around you but be inwardly transformed by the Holy Spirit through a total reformation of how you think,' (TPT).

2 Corinthians 10:3–7 'For though we live in the natural realm, we do not wage a military campaign employing human weapons, using manipulation to achieve our aims, instead our weapons are spiritual, energized with divine power to effectively dismantle the defences behind which people hide. We can demolish every deceptive fantasy that opposes God and break through every arrogant attitude that is raised up in defence of the true knowledge

of God. We capture, like prisoners of war, every thought and insist that it bow in obedience to the Anointed One,' (TPT).

Philippians 4:8–9 'And now, dear brothers and sisters, one final thing. Fix your thoughts on what is true, and honourable, and right, and pure, and lovely, and admirable. think about things that are excellent and worthy of praise. Keep putting into practice all you learnt and received from me and saw me doing. Then the God of peace will be with you,' (NLT).

# Chapter Thirteen

# The Spirit is Consciousness

*'For who knows a person's thoughts except their own spirit within them? In the same way, no one knows the thoughts of God except the spirit of God,'(NIV).*

## Introduction

*There are moments in life when we think we have found the treasure. Then there are other moments, albeit rarer, when we know we have.*

*As I was about to submit this manuscript to my publisher, I listened to a sermon on YouTube that had been first delivered by Charles Spurgeon over a hundred years ago.*

*The sermon was exploring the personality of the Holy Spirit.*

## The Holy Spirit

In his sermon, Spurgeon was stressing that the Holy Spirit was often considered a power flowing from God, perhaps as an attribute of God, whereas the Holy Spirit is a person, equally God with the Father and the Son.

As he quoted the passage from Paul's letter to the Corinthian Church, it was like God had placed the full stop at the end of my words, with a flourish. The great creator signed his approval in my mind with his light-pen.

His words gently caressed my mind, 'For who knows a person's thoughts except the spirit of that person, which is in him? So, no one comprehends the thoughts of God except the spirit of God.' My heart filled with gratitude. The search was over. I'd found treasure that buried deeper than the previous treasure I had found.

I introduced the Holy Spirit as consciousness in the previous chapter so here I just explore that a bit deeper and look at the practical implications of this in terms of the event cycle model.

This revelation introduces some new ways to illustrate our operating system using the event cycle.

**Event Cycle: The Unrenewed Habitual Mind**

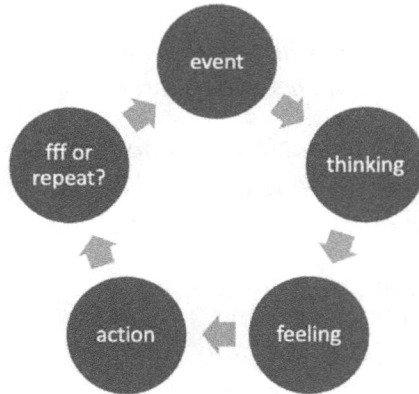

**Figure 10** The Simple Event Cycle 2

As illustrated by the standard event cycle process, normally we will perceive an event and immediately begin thinking about it. Depending on our personal frame of reference, we will give meaning to the event, often this is happening beyond our immediate awareness (consciousness).

The energy of the thought will begin to interact with our body and create feelings which will make the thought feel as if it is real, it has weight, so to speak. In habits, it is this weight which stimulates motivation either to go forward or retreat, both of which are actions.

The actions can either be attributed values, such as good or bad according to our personal preference, and sometimes the action is so habitual it happens despite our efforts to change or stop it, such as one of the three Fs of fight, flight, or freeze.

We can see in this model that actions are always motivated by personal thinking and so there is limited scope for change or fresh creativity.

In the psycho–spiritual model of principles-based psychology, we seek to interrupt the repeating patterns by using the event cycle model to notice where we can best interrupt according to our personality style, i.e., between the event and thinking, between thinking and feelings or between feelings and action (see chapter two).

As one of my clients put it, 'Interrupt the thought, cancel the feeling,' and that, for him, was his breakthrough moment.

**Event Cycle: The Biblical Model—Faith, Not Feelings**

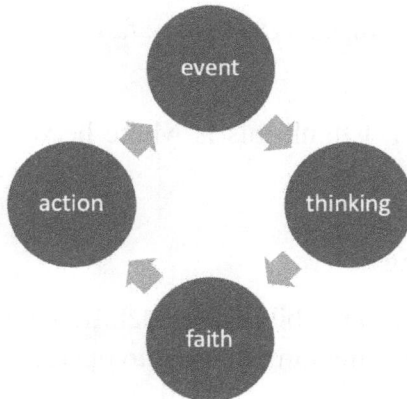

**Figure 11** The Event Cycle Faith Model

At first, this model might appear too simplistic to be practical but let's look at it in the context of Paul's New Testament teaching.

Even two thousand years ago, in so-called biblical times, there were events. They might not appear to be the same as we have now but, in their time, they were equally stimulating for the population of the era.

For example, as a Roman citizen one had to pay crippling taxes so an event might be having to queue at the tax booth after fishing all night, especially if the catch was small and the sales below target.

The patterns are the same, the times are different and when Paul said that we should not conform the patterns of the world, then that equally applies today.

So, in all human experiences, irrespective of the era in which the event occurs, we have just the same process. Human thinking occurs just the same because we are still on planet earth in earthly human bodies with an operating system calibrated to react or respond to what our senses detect coming from the environment.

But the Bible encourages us to live by faith, not by feelings (fear, doubt, worry).

According to Paul, I think this is where he would interrupt the event cycle.

## Faith, Not Feelings

Faith is not unique to the biblical model. In the human model we must have faith in something in order to operate at all.

For example, if I'm driving my car, I must have faith that the brakes are going to help me stop and if I'm taking a flight, I need faith in the pilot and the aircraft.

If I don't believe in a god of some sort, I have to have faith in myself because that's all I have!

Non-god faith must show up as faith in possessions and activities, and whatever we put our faith in, we give away our power too (see chapter seventeen, Are You Giving Away Your Power?).

Faith starts internally, as a pivotal foundation, a base value in our personal hierarchy of the way we give meaning to life.

Faith recalibrates our mind from natural to supernatural.

Paul states in 1 Corinthians 2:14, 'Someone living on an entirely human level rejects the revelations of God's spirit, for they make no sense to him. He can't understand the revelations of the Spirit because they are only discovered by the illumination of the Spirit,' (TPT).

For the spiritual person, faith is an integral part of the renewed mind's operating system and so we 'see' a different world, a world of security, of love and peace beyond the everyday events that would formally have created fear and insecurity.

The renewed mind has a fundamentally different way of processing events and so to be led by feelings is to compromise to one of the most powerful patterns of the world.

This is also because of the misunderstanding that our feelings are coming from our circumstances rather than our thinking.

How, then, do we control our habitual thinking responses?

Once again, Paul proves to be a psychologist as well as a spiritual teacher when he writes this in his second letter to the Corinthian

Church, 'We demolish arguments and every pretension that sets itself up against the knowledge of God, and we take captive every thought to make it obedient to Christ,' (NIV).

So, if we take every thought captive, see how that changes the flow of the event cycle—here is the perfect pattern interrupt, here is the key to the life of faith.

We need to take thoughts captive in the 'thinking' phase of the event cycle.

That is where we commune with the Holy Spirit and that is where we take the 'faith' route, talking care that we don't fall into the cul-de-sac of feelings!

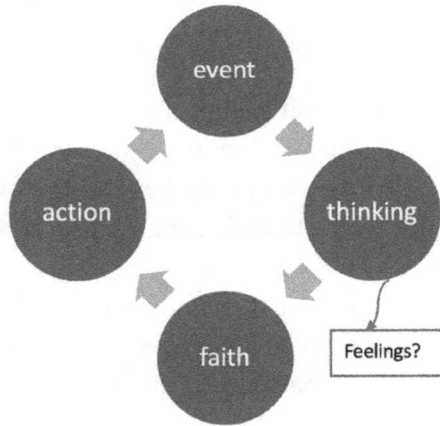

**Figure 12** The Event Cycle Faith and Feelings Model

## The Godhead, the Trinity in the Plan of Redemption

Paul was teaching a group of people who struggled with the patterns of their world—immorality, lying, cheating—all the stuff Jesus had said was not the way for humans to live.

Back in the earlier days, God had issued laws that, if followed strictly, would separate his chosen people from the world of destructive behaviour going on all around them.

They were unable to keep the law, so Jesus came to fulfil the requirements of that law in our place and took the punishment of that—death.

When Jesus returned to the Father, the Spirit came to indwell all those who accept the New Covenant of the Kingdom of God.

So, when Paul talks about obedience to Christ, he is also effectively saying obedience to the Holy Spirit.

Now it becomes more practical in day-to-day life because the Holy Spirit is operating in conjunction with our spirit, in our minds.

So how, in the event model, is faith a substitute for feelings?

We now see how we take our own thoughts captive and substitute faith in God, in His spirit and his word, the Bible.

We now have a new set of values operating in our minds.

If we continue to live by feelings we will be dragged about by popular opinion (pattern) and fashions (pattern) and other people's opinions (pattern).

Here is the perfect interrupt.

## The Spirit is Consciousness

This brings everything together and unifies our human and divine hybrid reality.

The mind is simply the place where we commune with God. Our spirit is the part of us that hears our thoughts and feels our feelings.

The human spirit and the human soul (our individuality) are invisible, our body is material, of the earth.

We are the place where God and human entwine.

When we accept Jesus Christ's substitutionary death and resurrection, the ascended Jesus gives us his spirit, entangled with ours.

In our mind we now have our human spirit enlivened by the spirit of God and our soul (heart) entwined with the soul of the first human to enter heaven, the Son of Man.

This is the renewed mind.

# Part Three

## Living with the Renewed Mind

***Introduction.*** *In Part One we looked at applications of the psycho–spiritual understanding of the mind called the Three Principles, or the inside-out model. Part Two brought the biblical teaching of the inside-out Kingdom of God's New Covenant with the world.*

*In Part Three we take the 'renewing of the mind' to the next level, looking at ways to recalibrate and live practically from day to day though the transition from the old me-first mind to the new supernatural, God-first mind.*

*Whether you're resisting the biblical guidance and opting instead for the earthly, humanistic, spiritual enlightenment route, I hope that you can use these strategies to break the patterns of the world and live life differently.*

*The inside-out revelation is not evolution, because evolution means that what we evolve from still exists (see monkeys for that one).*

*So, unless we still want the old mind to have some influence in our lives, we need to see this as a revolution and overthrow the old regime completely.*

*Humanistic enlightenment is one route, via spiritual principles. That's fine if you want to live a better life on planet Earth and then see what happens.*

*Godly enlightenment is a different route, described in the Bible, and is excellent if you'd prefer to be reunited with your creator and redeemer, live a life on Earth in the power of God's Holy Spirit and accept Jesus Christ's offer of eternal life.*

*Either way, it's your free choice.*

# Chapter Fourteen

# Our Spiritual Satnav

## Introduction

*We have been gifted with an internal navigation system based on spiritual algorithms a bit like the way Google works. I'll explain the difference between this worldly channel and God's supernatural guidance system.*

*Worldly wisdom is available to us all. There is a deeper mind, beyond the personal, habitual mind. A collaborative mind. Carl Jung referred to it as the collective unconscious.*

*We can use one of the awareness models or strategies set out in Part One such as the event cycle to interrupt our habitual thought/feelings to drop deeper and become aware of fresh thoughts, inspiration from beyond our own personal experience.*

*In this part I describe two strategies, Drop it! and Before Thought Begins, to connect to a deeper intelligence that is inherent in creation. This will help break the patterns and begin to recalibrate to a renewed mind, but it's not the mind of Christ.*

## We Need to Subscribe

To get access to God's satnav, which is the wisdom that comes from the mind of Christ, we need to subscribe to God's network.

People who don't believe in God are not given access to this network because it can only be received through the Holy Spirit in the heart because 'no one comprehends the thoughts of God except the spirit of God,' (1 Corinthians 2:11, ESV).

By accepting Jesus as our sin-sacrificial saviour, we are born again under God's New Covenant agreement and at that moment, the Holy Spirit engages with our spirit, enlivens it, tunes us into God's network and life is never the same again.

Now we have access to the spirit of truth, the spirit of wisdom, a supernatural service that is always online, unless we decide to terminate our subscription temporarily by not listening.

Involvement in the alternative spiritual models will interfere with our ability to connect to the Trinity's network.

If you don't know God, ask Jesus. Right now, tell him how sorry you are to have been part of the rebellion and accept by faith that the forgiveness he gave to all humans at the cross will be effective in your life.

Your subscription to God's satnav network will begin and you will have access to the mind of Christ and your life will change from the inside out.

This is the way the inside-out revelation works.

Meanwhile, if you subscribed or not, God still loves you, and I am making a way to be known to you, maybe through some of the following chapters.

Brave explorer, I challenge you now to read on.

### Using the Habitual Mind's Algorithms to Make Better Choices

Google is so unoriginal!

During my early work as a psychotherapist and personal development coach, I used NLP as a way of understanding the subjective human operating system.

I was especially fascinated with a function of the brain known as the reticular activating system (RAS).

The RAS operates in the subconscious part of our mental field, interacting with our mind in selecting specific data—information about the external environment—to which we need to give particular attention to in any given moment.

Every moment we are receiving masses of data via our senses and our personal operating system uses the preferences we have unconsciously installed during our life in selecting what we experience moment by moment. It filters out what we don't need to be aware of and brings to our awareness what will be useful for us.

Here we are reminded again of the inside-out mind because we use thought to process this data and our free will to make choices about actions we could take, our next step.

Depending on our individual state of mind, or level of consciousness at any given moment, we can be less or more aware of external data.

If we are stressed, we tend to have less capacity to process much, but when we have a clear, calm mind we can tolerate more. It might be true that those who are on the so-called spectrum of neurodiversity are aware of more or less data than the 'norm', if such a norm exists, but whatever level our personal system is set at, if we 'feel' as if we are exceeding our tolerance, then this causes further stress or anxiety.

If we believe that we must fit in with social and cultural norms, how society expects those patterns of the world, then our preferences will be different from someone who isn't so concerned about what others think. We also can find our preferences adjusting in different social situations, such as work or school where certain behaviours are expected, and compliance requires that we need to pay attention to different data.

So although many of our preferences might seem fixed, and those which go to make up our basic character or personality can become habitual, there is flexibility built into the system. The intelligence of our mind will adjust to how we can feel safe, accepted, and fit in.

When we have received God's Holy Spirit, the new mind is recalibrated to God's Kingdom, not the culture of the world from which God calls us out, and therefore it is easier for us to recognise how the Holy Spirit offers alternative patterns of thought and will recalibrate the RAS to 'see' a more beautiful reality.

## Flexibility of Thought

Creatives and artists are probably aware of more data options, and actors can adapt more easily to various roles, but the processing of incoming external data and innate habitual patterns is constantly happening, moment to moment.

The more we fall in with our mind's habitual thought patterns, the more restricted our bandwidth will be in filtering data of which we are aware.

If you find that your world has shrunk from a vast expanse of exciting potential to a little field of depressing problems, it might be time to change your mind from victim mode back to its natural creative mode.

How do we do that?

Here's a fun thought-experiment using the RAS.

You can programme your RAS by thought.

Think (say to yourself) that for the next few minutes you will see more red things in your visual field. Just think that with purpose, keep your eyes open and wait. As you scan your environment, red things will appear more obvious. I've done this and noticed a takeaway Coke cup someone's holding, a red scarf, red post box, red trousers on a woman in a painting on a coffee shop wall, and so on.

Next, close your eyes for a minute or two (to reset the RAS) and when you open them, think your RAS to select a different colour, any one you choose, and very probably it will obey, and you will become more aware of brown or green or yellow.

This part of the operating system works in a very similar way to how Google and all the other social media operatives select for us what they believe we want to see.

For example, I only need to mention Mick Jagger out loud in earshot of my smartphone and the next time I watch YouTube it's full of Rolling Stones videos.

I wonder, will the next step be Google et al. being able to select what I should be watching just by tuning into my thoughts?

So playing with the RAS gives us just a small example of our mind's role in selection, processing, and providing us with life options from moment to moment.

If we have such flexibility, only limited by the way we have innocently programmed our mind over time, then why not experiment with reprogramming and using the mind's natural creative potential to see more options than being restricted by a repetitive experience based on habitual thought patterns?

Once we see that our personal mind is really the principle of thought interacting with the brain, we have the key to working with the Holy Spirit to shift our realities and operate at a deeper level of love for the world and understanding of people's lost states.

## Algorithms of the Mind

The preferences that set our personal algorithms of the habitual mind are always operating, one hundred per cent perfectly, to create what we experience from moment to moment.

The only 'outer' influence is simply providing all the data the algorithm has available to select from in the moment, mixed with data in our personal memory.

The brain is part of the body and so is innocently conditioned by the outside-in operating model, and will maintain patterns that create thoughts and feelings about our survival and protection.

The brain matches patterns that are installed and imprinted like internal templates which match to the external environment (pattern recognition/matching) and this is why we respond or react to events by association.

This conditioning has no opinion as to whether anything is good or bad. It is literally machine-response to stimuli, and we are going along for the ride.

So the brain and personal habitual mind conspire to be as efficient as possible in maintaining patterns.

This means that if we come home after a stressful day, and patting our dog or cat gives us a feeling of relaxation, that will be installed as a habit that helps us and we will look forward to getting home to have that feeling again, every evening.

If our chosen relaxation stimulus is alcohol or cocaine, the same process occurs as the brain-mind has no awareness of the legal, cultural, or political consequences—it is down to our level of conscious awareness in managing that.

We will find it extremely difficult to renegotiate with our brain-mind through talking, especially considering that these patterns are held in place chemically. The Holy Spirit has the overriding power to interrupt our habitual algorithms if we give Him permission to do so.

So, we need to drop out of the worldly patterns, and this is where knowledge of this operating system is vital.

That's it, really. Personal memory recalls previous events but because time changes the way we feel these memories are often distorted and this contaminates the way we process the data, e.g. memories of life with an ex-loved one can play out in our mind alongside, or as a type of overlay, so we are living in a self-created perversion of what is simply happening.

Here's an analogy to try to illustrate how this works.

In a modern home we often have a central heating system which has a boiler and radiators that uses water, sometimes called a wet system. Pure, cold, clean water flows into the boiler which agitates it, causing it to heat up and the hot water flows into the radiators to heat the home.

In the human system, pure data flows into our personal mind and is agitated by our past preferences and flows into our awareness as useful to make our next choice.

But sometimes it's not so useful. Sometimes its assumption that what we want to experience contains painful memories that we just don't want to re-experience.

How can we tell our mind what we want, not what it thinks we want?

We do that in the thinking phase of the event cycle. This is where we pause, reflect, and bring the Holy Spirit and the Word of God into the cycle to take the faith route rather than drop into feelings and repeat habitual patterns.

If our life to date has programmed our mind to create repeat patterns of thought and behaviour, are we therefore now stuck in Groundhog Day?

Well, no, because we will continue to programme and reprogramme until we die so we must break the pattern through faith and different behaviour.

We can imagine all we want; we can huff and puff trying to materialise a different life but until we act, nothing will change.

Our mind hasn't been programmed by our thinking but by our doing.

If you want to break the habitual pattern of feeling safe when driving to work the same way every day, you must take a different route and the mind will adjust. Although it might feel odd, strange, and uncomfortable at first, the system will adapt and adjust.

You might find that you overwrite the previous one or create more options.

Installation happens through felt experience.

The principle of thought alone is not enough, it needs the spirit consciousness to bring thought alive, run it through the senses, embody the experience and install different wiring circuits.

## Worldly Patterns are Maintained by Algorithms.

Definition of mathematics: a set of rules for solving a problem in a finite number of steps, as the Euclidean algorithm for finding the greatest common divisor.

Computers use algorithms as an ordered set of intelligent instructions, recursively applied to transform data input into processed data output, as a mathematical solution, descriptive statistics, internet search engine result, or predictive text suggestions.

## Origin of Algorithms

The word 'algorithm' was first recorded in 1690-1700 and is a variant of algorism, the Greek arithmós or 'number'.

Definition of algorism: The Arabic system of arithmetical notation (with the figures one, two, three, etc.), the art of computation with the Arabic figures one to nine, plus the zero; arithmetic.

According to scholars, God's creation is based on mathematical laws of numbers that govern everything around us.

The complexity of the earth, as well as the immense expanse of space, proves that an intelligent being with tremendous power made them, but our limited perception of what's 'out there' doesn't always fit with the facts.

Have you ever 'seen' something that, when you get nearer to it, miraculously changes form into something else and you smile to yourself for being so stupid? How did I fall for that?

The 'snake' that is a rope?

The 'police speed check' that turns out to be some blue balloons on the front gate of a house announcing the location of a kid's party?

The 'old friend' walking towards you who turns out to be a total stranger bemused that you are beaming at them?

The 'injured cat' in the road ahead that turns out to be a supermarket bag?

Think about it. Let your RAS respond to your thinking and bring you back a memory or two and try not to snigger to yourself when you think of the times you were fooled by your perception.

So numbers sit beneath our perception and are an integral part of the universal system from which we create our own little corner of experience.

## Separate Realities

We are like 'mini gods', effectively but innocently programming our mind to create a reality that emerges as our experience according to our deepest desires. We can programme it consciously through different actions but if we don't, the habitual mind will create reality for us according to our defaults.

So align with God's Holy Spirit from moment to moment and reality will begin the shift from habit to inspiration.

Stop planning, start doing now, otherwise your mind will have you living out default patterns.

The mind hates a vacuum, so fill that vacuum with thought/ feelings and potential actions that align with your deepest desires, bearing in mind what that might mean if you want to fulfil God's plan for your life.

These moment-to-moment personal realities are not forever, and they will change according to the way we think, the way we use thought and consciousness from moment to moment, and act. God's plan, however, is always for our good and His purpose and so we recalibrate to the new mind and that is the mind of Christ.

'For I know the plans I have for you,' declares the Lord. 'Plans to prosper you and not to harm you, plans to give you hope and a future,' (Jeremiah 29:11, NIV).

God's internal satnav will reroute automatically, you won't get lost.

Unhappy? You get an unhappy reality.

Sad? You get a sad reality.

Think of yourself as stupid? You get a reality where you are stupid.

Think of yourself as clever? You get a reality where you can be the new Albert Einstein.

Little wonder we struggle to understand other people and get frustrated by their changing moods!

This is not magic, it's the operating system designed by a mind way more capable than any one mortal who has ever been grown on planet earth.

The numbers we discover related to our universe are so amazing that every human who understands them should conclude that God does exist (Romans 1:20).

In addition to this, the numbers in creation that we find use mathematical principles that offer a daily testament to the existence and power of a creator God!

## How Does Fear Stop Us Living Full Out?

If we are operating under the old, unrenewed mind, almost every choice and decision we make every day is influenced by the way we feel about our future.

We are constantly bombarded by media messages about future events with endless conjecture about what might happen.

Economic instability, disease and war is at our door. It's only a matter of time.

Behind the scenes our innate sensors are picking up these danger signals and although we are unaware of it, background levels of anxiety about our future security are on high alert.

It's a bit like the UK terror alert, which varies in intensity according to the intelligence that the authorities are aware of. We are not informed about what threatens the security of our country or state for our own good, so we can 'keep calm and carry on' but the threat is enough for it to be hinted at with a media-released security-level warning.

So similarly, our internal systems are always operating, always alerting us to the environment we are living in. By that I mean the unseen energetic environment created by those around us including the media messages.

Our feelings are the indicator of that underlying, unseen, energetic environment—some might call it a 'vibe' but wherever you call it, we are affected by it daily.

It happens that sometimes our awareness of the underlying anxiety is heightened, and we get a warning such as heightened feelings or a sense that something isn't right. Some call it a feeling of dread that comes from nowhere.

This process works in a similar way in our physical bodies.

When we get a pain in the body, that is making us aware that we might need to change what we are eating, drinking, or the way we are sitting, or it might be a more significant issue.

The thing is that the body has already been attempting to adjust and remedy the issue before we are made aware of it by a pain signal.

There is so much going on behind the scenes both physically and psychologically, and it's beneficial to be aware of this when it could potentially threaten our wellbeing and ability to perform at our best.

What do we do?

I want to let you in on a secret that this is all about the way we experience our environment, and this will help you to conquer a very real source of anxiety.

I'll start with an example.

Have you ever been to a big theme park such as Disney or Alton Towers? Kids love these places and especially the big rides.

The truth is that we like to push our fear buttons. We get a thrill out of challenging those innate alarms to see how far we can go. We need to test our limits and we can do that at a fun park because that's what we perceive it as—fun.

When we are taking on a new business venture or introducing a new initiative to boost our business, we treat that differently.

That is real, so maybe we pull back and compromise.

That is because of this trick of the unrenewed mind which manifests while we are waiting in the queue for the next big ride.

When we are waiting in the queue our In-perception® systems are on full alert to the potential dangers and we can do very little about it. There are no techniques or tricks that work every time.

We are feeling the situation in our bodies irrespective of what we are thinking. Changing your personal thinking about the situation will make very little difference.

The chemicals being injected into your nervous system by your brain, as it anticipates possible outcomes, are creating feelings of fear, excitement, anticipation, making you feel like you want to run, get on quicker, freeze, run again—so much going on and all you are doing is standing in a queue. There is nothing going on other than your imagination 'overlaying' what you see with multiple possibilities and the likelihood is that none of them will actually happen as you imagine.

Your felt experience when you are on the ride will be totally different from the confusion of imagined experiences you are creating in your mind while in the queue.

This is just how we operate within our environment as humans so there is nothing wrong and nothing you need to do other than to know and be aware of what's going on.

What happens if the feelings you are getting in the queue become so uncomfortable that you must leave, and you never take the ride?

You run away and get a doughnut.

After a while the feelings subside as the chemicals dissipate into your bloodstream and your body cleans them out.

Then you get that little voice in your head telling you what a wimp you are and how stupid you've been, and you will probably even get the urge to go back and have another go, rejoin the queue because the next time it will be different.

That is just a fun fair. That is just ridiculous—isn't it?

There is a wealth of material here for a stand-up comedy routine because we all know what it's like to fear ourselves. We can all relate to this.

That enlightened philosopher Sydney Banks, was just an ordinary human like you and me, who had an extraordinary experience of understanding how life works said, 'If the one thing people learnt was not to be afraid of their experience, that alone would change the world.'

We are not afraid of life itself; we are never afraid of reality itself.

That is because we are simply afraid of our experience of reality and the way every one of us experiences reality is unique to us if we are operating from the me-first mind.

Our greatest source of fear is us and it arises from the legacy mind.

The unrenewed mind will try to persuade us that greatest source of everything we need to overcome fear is also ourselves, but it's not, it's our God who promises to never leave us or forsake us.

This is how the unrenewed mind works to trap us in unreal fear. Let's bring Disney World into the sales office. I'm not suggesting that you rebrand as Disney Sales but that you look at the process that happens at the big ride and map it across to your experience of a day in the life of the owner of an independent estate agency.

What is the reason we run from getting on the ride?

Fear of our own experience of the ride. Never the ride itself. When we're in the ride it feels different because we are experiencing the event live and interactive, with feedback from the interaction, and however good our imagination is, we can never experience that feedback loop before or after any real event. It just doesn't work that way.

When you are preparing to call a prospect, you are not experiencing the call itself and you are not feeling how you will feel when you are on the call.

You are feeling where you are right at that moment—thinking about making the call—and in that moment all the different possibilities are playing out in your personal thinking, and you are overloading on what-ifs, like watching multiple news channels at the same time.

So, what is the answer?

Just make the call.

Most successful performers, whether in sport or the arts, will tell us that they perform at their best when they are in the flow or the zone. That flow and zone rarely happens when they are thinking about the race or the show. It's in the moment that they flow.

Here's the key to this: There are always two elements to an event. There's the rehearsal, the practice, the pre-run or whatever you want to call it. We love to do that and if we are learning a skill, it's good to practice the moves.

In sales you will have practiced your moves, but the real juice comes in the moment of your experience, real and live and getting feedback.

When we really get this, it changes everything.

It is fear stops us from getting on the ride.

### Fear of *future danger*

We don't take the ride because we are afraid of future danger.

We run away because of our fear of our imagined future danger.

The danger is self-created and projected from us where we are now in the queue into a future that can never exist if we never take the ride.

Fact: The danger we are afraid of can never exist if we don't take the ride.

Because we never take the ride.

If we never take the ride, we will never experience the event which we fear.

How will we know how it will turn out if we don't take the ride?

Faith, not fear!

### The Iceberg Metaphor

There's a metaphor sometimes used in counselling or psychotherapy concerning the theory of our mind having two parts: a conscious and subconscious.

In this metaphor, the conscious is what we are aware of in any given moment, whereas the subconscious, sometimes called the 'unconscious', is like a vast storage container of all our memories, habits, routines, beliefs, and maybe, even deeper, a collective of all human desires and drives.

Psychologist Carl Jung talked about archetypes and Freud was convinced that early years' experience set our sexual drivers in the subconscious.

We can only retain a small amount of information in our conscious awareness so it's a bit like the working memory of a computer. The subconscious is our storage, the hard drive, as it were, so at times we can dip into that storage to recall information in deep storage.

I agree with the metaphor but not with the theory. In a mind that is operating by principles of thought and consciousness (or spirit) with the event cycle as our guide, then, after an event has triggered the cycle, we are aware of it, and we know that we will either run a habitual routine or we can interrupt and drop into faith, where we will be aware of a different quality of thought.

The event cycle takes away the mystery of mind and the danger of the unknown subconscious and this gives us access to more power, wisdom, control, and mastery in the operating system.

So, if we apply the event cycle to the iceberg metaphor, it can appear more helpful and give us more personal control.

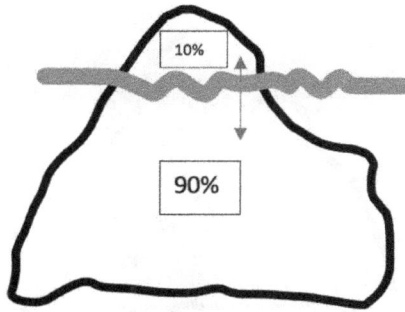

**Figure 13** The Habitual Mind Iceberg

In the habitual mind iceberg, the ten per cent above the 'waterline' is our conscious mind and the ninety per cent below the waterline represents our subconscious.

The small arrow represents the mind's moment-to-moment 'dipping down' from conscious to subconscious to bring up relevant information into our awareness.

If we apply the event cycle, then the event will be above the waterline, thinking will be a mix of conscious and subconscious, feeling will result from the thinking and our action will also then be above the waterline.

This metaphor assumes that the human mind works as a closed system. By this I mean that we are only ever operating from what we know, from our previous experience. There is no real understanding of insight and inspiration falling into our awareness from God or the universe, depending on your version of spirituality.

So, a post-paradigm iceberg metaphor would now recognise that the iceberg is not self-contained at all but is frozen in a moment of time, made up of the surrounding water within which it is floating.

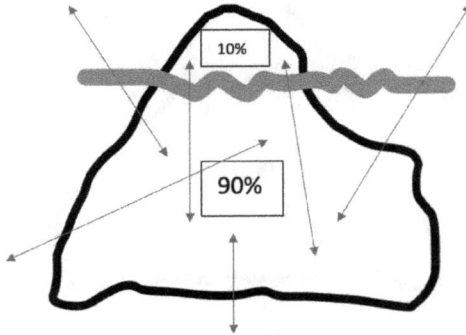

**Figure 14** The Renewed Mind Iceberg

Now we see that we have two-way flow of intelligence from within the iceberg as we recognise that everything in the image is made of the same source material, but just appearing in different form, just as all matter behaves.

The surrounding water is fluid and without form, whereas the iceberg is the same water but in form for a period before it becomes formless and fluid once more.

In the biblical version, God's Holy Spirit is both in the external environment as the spirit of the creator God sustaining the world and simultaneously inside our operating system connecting us to the source. We can't lose, God speaking to God with 'us' almost as bystanders with the privilege of taking the action that God decides for the benefit of the world.

## Inside-Outside Window

Once we've realised the inside-out nature of the mind, it's a wonderful experience to begin to practice spending time opening up the space inside, the space between thoughts, the space before feelings arise (where we exercise our faith) or the space between thought/feeling and actions.

In this illustration, the window represents the percentage of the time that the mind is using memory as the primary reference for making decisions in the present moment, as opposed to fresh insights from the deeper mind or the Holy Spirit. For example, in the first window we are only ten per cent likely to have fresh ideas. The aim of the exercise is to open up to fresh insights most of the time so that we are led by wisdom or the spirit of God to be more creative and enjoy new experiences.

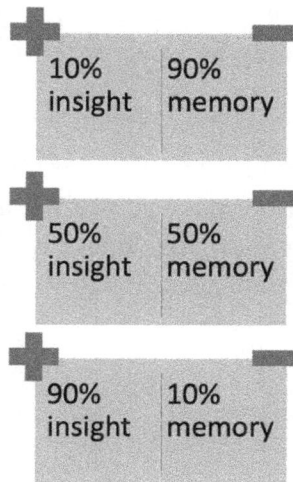

**Figure 15** The Inside-Outside Window

If we use that iceberg model as a guide, with only ten per cent of our awareness above the waterline, we need a target to open our 'window of awareness' and fifty per cent can be achievable.

We are looking for fifty per cent insight and inspiration for any given event, rather than ninety per cent of our responses being habitual.

Imagine being able to open your communication with Holy Spirit in this way?

## A Reminder That We Need to Subscribe

As I mentioned at the start of this chapter, to get access to God's satnav, which is the wisdom that comes from the mind of Christ, we need to subscribe to God's channel.

People who don't believe in God are not given access to this service because it can only be received through the Holy Spirit in the heart.

By accepting Jesus as our saviour, we are born again and at that moment the Holy Spirit, God's counsellor, advocate, and guide, installs himself in your spirit and your new mind is activated.

# Chapter Fifteen

# Before Thought Begins

## Communing with the Holy Spirit

*'But when the Spirit of truth comes, he will guide you into all the truth,' (John 16:13, NIV).*

## Introduction

*Renewing the mind is an inside job. Once we change the operating system, what we see outside has a different effect on us because, like sonar, we perceive what we believe. Once we've learnt the old habitual mind's strategy of keeping us busy with constant flows of earthbound thoughts based on the past and an imaginary future, we can find mental health and emotional wellbeing literally in the present moment.*

*This chapter includes ideas I was practicing with clients, helping them to find that space away from the hamster wheel of busyness. I have now reframed what was a psychological concept into a psycho–spiritual practice and added communion with the Holy Spirit into the mix!*

*The whole point is to help us to escape the entrapment of the unregenerate, unruly, stubborn, earthbound mind and find eternal life through the joy of the renewed mind.*

## Unhelpful Narrative

Most people I have worked with find that to ignore the unrenewed mind's narrative is more helpful than trying to negotiate with it.

The only reason we think that the unrenewed mind's chatter is important is because we hear it in a voice that has become very familiar, almost comforting, even though we might have chosen to no longer obey what it suggests.

That's the point, in a way, isn't it? That unregenerated mind's tactical approach is to suggest things. It suggests that 'there' is better than 'here' or 'they' are better than 'me' and so on.

The subtle doubts, the gentle nudges, they are so tempting. Reflect on that for a moment!

I offer you, in both the BTB and Drop it! strategies, practices that will help to break the pattern of internal chatter and release the power of God's inspiration.

BTB helps us to locate and be in the space where we can hear fresh and inspired thoughts arising about subjects and objects that our old narrative tries to cast influence over.

In the event cycle model, the phase this takes place is after the event and just before the thinking phase starts.

This is the dwelling space where recalibration miracles can happen, from the inside out.

**The Inner Space**

As we've already been reminded, the Apostle Paul wrote to the community of believers in his letter entitled Romans, 'Be no longer conformed to the patterns of the world but be transformed by the renewing of your mind.'

That's what this book and the inside-out revelation has been all about.

I really don't mind how you see your status with God, whether you think you're 'saved' or 'redeemed' or 'one of the elect'. My reason for writing is to ask you to join a revolution in putting an end to the tempting inner voice of the unrenewed mind that causes us so much worry, stress, anxiety and consequently, the doubt and fear that infects our minds and hearts.

The 'patterns of the world' that Paul referred to can still be seen, heard, and experienced in human activity throughout the world, flowing from the sinful nature, manifesting from mind to body and displayed in such attitudes as jealousy, judgement, criticism, and competition.

Despite our best efforts so far, as leaders in Bible-focused wellbeing, we have compromised through our benevolence to these attitudes, maybe as just accepting them as that's the way the world works, and maybe we've personally done our best to 'live in the world, but be not of the world' as Jesus taught, but that's not really good enough, is it, because we still see so many Christians in our churches increasingly stressed, worried, anxious, and fearful, unable to live out the life for which we want and hope.

If a born-again spiritual life is not working out and Christians are turning to psychology, psychotherapy, psychiatry, and secular life coaching then I'm convinced that the availability of a different type of psychology should not be ignored.

I'm offering Christians, whatever their spiritual 'status', a different psychology, a spirituality-based psychology, one that I've found is much more appropriate to the Christian life than the Freudian, humanistic psychology of the past 150 years that has taken us away from God rather than closer.

Would God have intended us to get born again, given a new nature, and then go for a few sessions of psychiatry or psychotherapy? That strategy doesn't appear in the New Testament.

It breaks my heart, the number of young people in churchgoing families that I've known since I became a Christian in 1988, who have been in rehab, institutions, mental health centres, often drugged up to the eyeballs with legal medication that has dulled and depressed their minds.

Why have we, as influencers, allowed this to be in any way acceptable?

God has revealed that we have been living with a misunderstanding about what the mind is and how it works and is now illuminating through the world of psychology a life-changing revelation. When we realise the truth of how the mind works (the inside-out model) this brings freedom from worry, stress, and anxiety, even to the unregenerated mind.

When lived according to the way the operating system is designed, our life becomes a very different experience, we can be enjoying every moment irrespective of our circumstances, finances, relationships or the size of our house or car.

We find space to commune with God's Holy Spirit, even in the busyness of everyday life. It brings God home to us, reduces the gap and blows away the deception that God is a sort of Father Christmas for grown-ups.

This inside-out understanding is for everyone, irrespective of age, brain power, physical condition, culture, place of birth, colour, in fact any intellectual outside-in barrier you can think of that has obstructed unity and the communion of not just the saints, but of whole societies.

To realise this inside-out revelation comes by way of insight—that's a sight from within—not from the level of intellectual 'cleverness' that has created and thrived in this misunderstanding about the mind, kept us in a darkness, enforced through our outside-in education system, culture, and especially media.

## A Different Operating Model

Due to the fact that many churchgoing believers are still struggling with the stress that arises from the old mind, I'm suggesting that some people might need to recalibrate initially to a different operating model even before they can fully enjoy the renewed mind.

This inside-out mind model is almost like an upgrade that has been provided by God to help us navigate these difficult times.

A lot of people comment that time seems to be speeding up. Information is flooding our minds, we are aware of failing political and social systems across the world, not just locally, and we are deluged with global troubles.

When Jesus was on earth he talked of news of wars, famine, earthquakes, but he could have been giving the people of 2,000 years ago a prediction of a future global shakedown such as we are seeing and hearing about every day through the news media.

## Enlightenment from the Inside Out

It turns out that rather than having to travel the world to find ourselves, we already have within us everything we need to navigate this fallen world as we await the Lord's return or it's our personal time to leave earth.

The psycho–spiritual tools we need to realise the inside-out revelation have always been available in the intelligence of

God's creative design of nature through the Holy Spirit but due to the inherent spiritual blindness of the unrenewed mind, they have been occluded until now.

Now they are revealed, we find them necessary to realise the innate health we all have hard-wired into our human operating system.

Christian community, we must set aside our religious thinking and our insecurities that keep us trapped in the old nature and recalibrate to this very different operating model.

To begin the recalibration, we need to find some space in our busy mind that is deeper than the habitual, repetitive, programmed conditioning that maintains the outside-in model of the unrenewed mind, that persuades us that we are lost, isolated and alone in the world.

## The Power of Principles

Some people are fortunate to have 'enlightenment' experiences which wake them from the sleepy, always the same, earthbound, me-first mind, and they 'see' life a different way.

There have been many during the past two thousand years and Jesus was often thought be another one of them, rather than the divine presence on earth.

However, for most of us, waking up takes longer, maybe a lifetime!

If we are using psychology as a method to effect change, up to the paradigm shift of the principles basis, we have been offered over six hundred theories to choose from, on how the mind works.

As these theories emerge and their practitioners promote them as the next great discovery, we have tried and failed to find one that really makes any difference.

The fundamental problem is that we haven't had principles that ground theories in science or fact.

The unrenewed earthbound mind has had us resist spiritual truths, but for over fifty years, spiritual principles have been introducing to the world the new paradigm of spirituality-based psychology. I see this as the bridge between the pre-principles humanistic theories about the mind and the new mind of the inside-out Kingdom.

Miracles of instantaneous enlightenment do occur, but as a way of transitioning and recalibrating from earthbound to Kingdom-bound mindsets, these principles are assisting people across the globe to wake up.

A principle is a fact that is true, irrespective of whether we personally believe it or not.

There has been a 'gap' between God and humans created in the fallen mind. Our culture has characterised God as an old man in the sky who popped up as a bearded wanderer on the earth 2,000 years ago but, more recently, an old-fashioned joke, a concept.

What has also not been an acceptable image is a God who is active today, does different things, who goes before us, and then waits for us to catch up. Jesus displayed this characteristic during his time on earth—he went before the disciples during his mission and promised to prepare a place for them in 'His Father's mansion'.

The trouble is, like the disciples after Jesus had risen, we get bored waiting for him to reappear and go back to our 'fishing'.

With the uncovering of psycho–spiritual principles of the mind, God has done it again and prepared a way for us to be in communion with him every moment of every day, in a much closer way, a realistic, appropriate, and fun way. A way not dependent on talking in a language more suited to medieval times, not grounded in the Welsh revival, not part of the Toronto blessing or the old charismatic movement.

God has been revealing himself recently in technology, in social media, through brain scanning, the discovery of neuroplasticity, quantum mechanics, and now, as if to take a complete U-turn from the outside-in deception, he's revealed spiritual principles for life that form our psychological experience here on planet earth.

## The Inside-Out Principles of the Mind

A realisation for anyone, of any culture and education, that the principles of divine mind, consciousness, and thought are the spiritual tools that God has revealed for humanity at this time in history is revolutionary.

That God has given us the gift of tools that enable us to see beyond our preconceived outside-in conditioning, to recognise the patterns of this world for what they truly are—deceptive, destructive, and based on a very clever lie—is the breakthrough we all need.

God has revealed that we have these psycho–spiritual gifts that will guide us and help us.

This is the bridge, the missing link between the visible dimension of earth and the invisible dimension of heaven.

We have, after all, unlimited access to divine mind, a mind that is vastly bigger and more powerful to change our destiny and more accessible than we have been led to believe.

We have all innocently set our minds to work the outside-in model which is founded on us assuming that we are lost individuals searching for something 'out there' to complete us, separate from all nature and competing for limited resources.

It's all a subtle lie of the tempter.

To access the divine super-mind, with its power to renew our personal, habitual mind's outside-in conditioning, we need to go deeper than our personal intellectual understanding and allow a deeper consciousness to arise.

## Interpretations of the Principles

The principles of mind consciousness and thought are metaphors to describe the intelligent energy which empowers our human operating system. As they are spiritual, they are invisible and formless.

The fact is that we are aware (conscious), we think, and we have a mind in which we undertake this activity.

However, if we take Paul's teaching in his letter to the Corinthians that 'No one understands the thought of a man except the spirit of a man,' this rebrands consciousness as Spirit and so for Christians, the principles become mind, *spirit*, and thought.

This brings spirit 'home' from somewhere out there, to right inside our mind as the observer of our thoughts.

## Bringing it All Together

As we have seen in Part Two, all of these operating tools are widely referred to in the Bible throughout all of God's covenant agreements with His people, but mostly in the New Testament where we have the new, inside-out Kingdom covenant.

I'm happy to use the principles as a basis for exposing the old mind and transitioning to the new one as long as we use them in accordance with biblical teaching.

## The Principles in Action

Firstly, as we get started with our recalibration, we need to become more aware of the habitual outside-in thought patterns that keep us in the outside-in model.

Using the event cycle model, we can see how to be aware of our habitual thought patterns as they arise, and see that we have a choice to break those patterns and engage the Holy Spirit's unlimited creative process instead.

One of the incorrect and deceptive beliefs about our operating system has persuaded us that we are in our physical head and that assumption is extremely limiting. If we see instead that our head is part of the whole body/mind, part of the mysterious space where we communicate with God's divine intelligence that pervades all creatures on this planet, we begin to shift to a more expansive experience, joining with the nature of God through the principles.

God, as the creator of all things, is here. It is God's mind and Paul personalised this further by referring to it as the mind of Christ.

## Getting Started in the Basics

We can become more deeply conscious of the space that exists in our experience for fellowship with the Holy Spirit before the automatic old mind cycle kicks in and we become absorbed in our conditioned personal thinking.

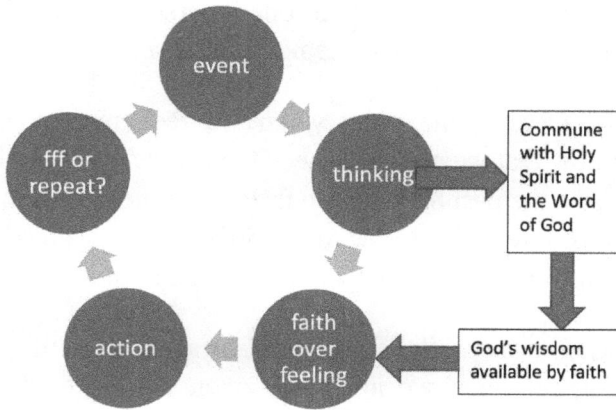

**Figure 16** The Event Cycle: BTB Communing Model

The event is any stimulus, and our automatic inner response is always filtered through our thinking, which is based on our personal preferences, previous experience, and safety-first programming.

This is the first point where we can decide to be conscious of the Holy Spirit's guidance instead.

Once we realise that thinking always follows events, then we can understand that feelings are not random, nor are they directly arising from the event itself, but intrinsically linked to thought. And here is another point where we have a choice to be conscious of the Holy Spirit's intelligence instead.

By practicing being conscious of the Holy Spirit's presence in the cycle, we can interrupt the pattern of personal habitual thinking and will be open to have new insights and fresh thoughts about the event.

I've found that this might take a while because the personal mind's conditioning can be very deeply embedded and if we find that we are still stuck in the conditioned, personal reactions, there are still other opportunities to break the pattern.

Specifically, there is the point when we feel motivated to act. Conscious now that we no longer need to be a victim of our habitual feelings that in the past have driven us to the options of fight, flight, freeze, or repeat, we can decide to not do anything or do something completely different as we are inspired by God's spirit.

Divine thought from the mind of Christ is free of personal conditioning so when we are more open to this fresh, in-the-moment guidance, we also no longer feel isolated. With experience, we will find that we can trust the Lord through the divine thought and consciousness principles to have our back and provide wisdom and knowledge way beyond our personal conditioned me-first mindsets.

Our existing state of mind affects our awareness of the event cycle.

It's vitally important to understand how our moment-to-moment experience of events as they are happening is going to be affected and potentially dulled if we are in a state of worry, stress, anxiety, and depression.

The event cycle illustrates that it's our personal thinking that always follows any event and is the missing knowledge that helps to maintain the outside-in misunderstanding.

If we erroneously assume that our feelings are the direct result of the event, then we will be victims of the events, unable generally to take control of life's circumstances.

The outside-in model of circumstances creating feelings is persuasive because we have innocently programmed our personal operating system to protect us from events and have not acknowledged or trusted the divine in the system. We tend to have a negative bias based on me-first, insecure programming which is why our internal commentary is so often negative and we wonder why.

Outside-in thinking takes us away from the divine state of innate wellbeing that exists in the inside-out revelation because of the worry, stress, and anxiety that arises as we try to make sense of an outside-in world, so we can be blind to new ideas, absorbed with the fear of isolation, loss, and insecurity.

This is one of the reasons why sometimes we find it more difficult to be 'outside' of the cycle, in the Spirit, being the observer, hanging out in the space where we have a moment to make different choices.

## Gear Shift—Realising Neutral Exists

While we are absorbed in stressed, outside-in thinking, it's not easy to shift directly into a calmer state. When circumstances seem to conspire, when relationships falter, when health is threatened, we must stay in the truth of God's word by faith.

Peace, but not as the world offers it.

'Be still and know that I am God,' (Psalm 46:10, NIV).

By way of illustration, think of the gear shift in a motor car. Even if we have an automatic car, to move from one gear to another there must be a moment when the gears shift through neutral.

Immediately following an event, as soon as we are aware of our involvement in something, that is the time to go into neutral where the Holy Spirit is waiting in the peace, ready with fresh inspiration aligned with God's word and the plan He has for us.

Once we relax and become aware that it is never the event to which we are responding right now, but our thinking about the event, we can see our role in renewing the mind, and all we must do is tune into the Holy Spirit rather than trust our own intellect. 'Trust in the Lord with all of your heart and lean not on your own understanding,' (Proverbs 3:5, NIV).

Even these words you are reading are an event, which we must think about, to give meaning to, to feel and act. If we think these words are rubbish, we might feel like we're wasting our time and put the book down. If instead we drop our personal thinking, then that removes any personal meaning, then we are much freer to try this new way and see for ourselves if it might help us to engage with life differently.

So, what happens if we are overwhelmed by multiple events?

A few years ago, I was hosting a group session to explore the event cycle. One of the participants arrived late and was clearly in a state of anxiety. I asked if she would like to tell us what had happened to see if we could help her calm down. She said that three events had occurred that morning and she felt the universe was conspiring against her.

She sat down and recalled that she had woken up late and didn't have time to shower, she received a text from a friend saying that he had been diagnosed with cancer, and then driving to the session, she'd had an accident with another car.

When her mind calmed down, she could see that her personal me-first mind was telling her the events were conspiring, all about her, creating feelings of anger, frustration, and anxiety. She hadn't had time to act on the events because of the need to get to the session on time which was the meta-event that was affecting all these other events.

She began to see that it was her habitual thinking that was creating her anxiety and each event could be better managed by separating them and dealing with the process with a calm mind, fresh thinking, and a different level of consciousness to connect to universal choices.

I refer to this process of overwhelm by a commonly used but misunderstood term 'overthinking', which is caused by a misunderstanding and improper use of the principle of thought.

Thinking is a mental process, but it involves the whole body when, as the cycle illustrates, the principle of consciousness through the Spirit energises our thoughts, brings them alive and we feel that energy as emotion in our body.

This is the way our thoughts directly influence our perception and become real enough to literally change the way we experience our reality in the moment.

Without understanding this process, we can become stressed and anxious and stuck in a state of mind that is unhelpful and painful.

This is because our perception of events is through an ever-changing state of mind which is constantly affecting the way we experience the environment, and this influences our relationships and our productivity, due to these unpredictable mood swings leading to unreliability.

Overthinking causes the overwhelm and the whole operating system over works, which can lead to system stress which eventually causes some form of shutdown procedure.

At this stage of the process, we often attempt to create an escape route from the thought-pollution that's infecting our system, and this is where our habitual coping mechanisms such as alcohol, drugs, internet and TV addiction kick in.

Often the 'bad' habits we later try to stop have become an integral part of our personal mind's preferences as coping mechanisms, which is why it can be so difficult to stop them. The mind has accepted them, not as good or bad, but just because they make us feel better and the mind assumes that's what we want.

This is why dropping into the space before thought begins cuts off personal thinking before it can create feelings and we take the faith option.

Our personal mind is constantly in a state of flux, reacting to events, whereas the divine mind is constant, neutral, creative, and relevant because it is the cause rather than the effect.

We use God's constant creative power to move to our next event rather than trying to fix the present one.

If you are baking a cake and it comes out burnt, you can scrape off the burnt bits and make the best of it or throw it away and start again with fresh ingredients.

That is the life in the principles. We always have fresh ingredients at our disposal and the principles are always creating fresh.

## Dropping out of the Event Cycle

The system works perfectly, but it's working on an incorrect assumption—the outside-in misunderstanding, so we need to use our free will to break out of a situation that is seemingly unresolvable.

It's due to a lack of understanding as to how the mind's processes work that allows us to misuse the principles and this can allow misthinking in our system.

Correcting any innocent misunderstanding we have about the mind's processing will help us gain mastery and open far more choices.

So, a reminder: Worry is overthinking about unresolved events.

Stress is caused by us trying to solve an event using old actions that are inappropriate for the present event.

Anxiety is being stuck in the loop of multiple unresolved events, much like a hamster on a wheel.

Depression arises as a feeling of being under this unresolved event-stack with no apparent escape, so the system is automatically shutting down, but it feels like we are losing control.

Whether it's worry, stress, anxiety, or depression we can run this through the event cycle to see where we can intervene.

To do this effectively, we need to be outside of the loop, an observer, an operator rather than the operation itself, the author rather than a character in the play.

## The Boxer

In a boxing match, when the bell rings to start the bout, the boxer rises from their seat in their corner and enters the contest.

The contest is broken into short sessions called rounds and between each round is a space to enable the boxers to rest, regroup and take on in-the-moment guidance and advice from their trainers, who are called 'seconds'. After the allotted rest time, the referee calls 'seconds out' which means that they literally must leave the ring, and the next round commences.

265

This continues until either boxer has won, or the fight ends for a points decision.

So why doesn't the fight just run for thirty minutes without breaks?

It's because it's a tactical game based on breaking down the whole into parts.

Understanding the rules and the structure of the game is basically about survival.

The skill is then how to box, how to win.

## The Hamster

The hamster on its wheel is running a loop, a repeat pattern. To escape the loop, there will come a moment when the hamster slows down due to exhaustion or throws itself off the wheel to scurry to the opposite corner of the cage to get water.

We have a natural way to break the pattern of the habitual, conditioned, survival-based event-thought-feeling-action cycle.

The observer is the human spirit, nothing more, nothing less, but Jesus promised that we will receive power when the Holy Spirit comes upon us. (Acts 1:8.)

The Holy Spirit is God's water to quench our thirst for new life, and this is His promise to us so let's take up the opportunity and enjoy the peace and inspiration of the creator's presence in all of our life events.

# Chapter Sixteen

# Drop it! Mental Health in a Moment

## Introduction

*For a few years now there has been a big debate about the nature of mental health. Social media is full of ideas and there are often special days dedicated to awareness, happiness, clear-thinking and so on. You might find that the previous chapter, BTB, helped calm your busy mind and find the Holy Spirit in each event. The next chapter follows a very similar theme but rather than seeking to dwell in the space between thoughts, Drop it! is a strategy to literally drop out of the unrenewed mind into a deeper communion with the spirit when we find that we are listening to the wrong voice.*

*I wrote Drop it! during the first lockdown in 2020 when my mind kept wandering off into a cloud of 'what if?' and 'how come?', you know the type of thing it tries to feed us on? I truly believe that we have innate mental health, but we think our way out of it. Drop it! is designed to reset our inmate wellbeing and realign with God's plan.*

## *Sat Nag?*

*I'm aware myself of being nagged by my own mind! The incessant chatter and constant commentary in my head often affects my ability to concentrate on tasks in hand and so, inspired by one particular mental health awareness day, I began to explore ways to manage or change the way I could relate to my 'motor mind' that could potentially help my clients as well.*

*I was at a time in life when my circumstances meant that I was alone a lot of the time with my thinking. I was between relationships, living on my own, and my mind was working overtime coming up with possible scenarios as to what might happen to me.*

*I knew that my mind was being creative and positive, but my prevailing emotional state was the opposite and quite unstable, and I just wanted some peace and quiet.*

*I came up with the Drop it! strategy while watching a YouTube video of a Bible-based teacher who specialised in renewing the mind, and the words I heard that inspire this strategy went something like this: 'When it's unhelpful to listen to my own mind, I just go unconscious!'*

*What did that mean, how was it possible? It sounded plausible, but did it mean just dropping asleep?*

*This chapter is a copy of the Drop it! strategy that I wrote in 2020 for general use. Clients have found it helpful to interrupt their event cycle when they realise that they are stuck in the loop of memory-based unhelpful thoughts, feelings, or behaviour.*

## Drop it! Mental Health in a Moment

### Identifying the Target

What is your idea of perfect mental health?

To hit a target, we need to know what the target looks like, where it is located and what resources we will need to achieve it.

Here are four questions to consider before we start:

What is your personal mental health target?
What does it look like?
Do you know where to find it?
What resources will you need to achieve it?

In other words, what is your personal model of the mental health you want for yourself?

As a psychotherapist I've found that clients bring a variety of problems into consultation but there are some issues that are common to all, and overthinking is the most troublesome.

Consider now, what are your personal issues that you have struggling with?

Intrusive thoughts?
Overthinking?
Unwanted feelings?
Tired and irritable?
Unable to concentrate?
Loneliness?
Fear of the future?
Suicidal thoughts?

These are just a few of the unwanted symptoms that clients have indicated to me. They are manifestations of the old fallen legacy mind that has these aspects within its operating system by nature.

Although the unwanted issues seem to be quite easily listed, the desired outcomes are often not so clear and tend to be less defined, but in most cases I would suggest some of these:

Clear mind.
Calm feelings.

Contentment.
Self-confidence.
A lightness and humour.
Easy relationships.
Unconditional love and acceptance.

By the way, in all my years of experience I've found that there is no right model for mental health outside of the biblical model, which is why that one seems to make sense over and above all the other ideas and concepts of what life is about and what we are all up to.

Think about it. Is there one human being who displays a perfect model of mental health that the industry is trying to sell to us? The more we explore this, the more the current proposals for mental health just don't reach the target.

In fact, generally we don't have a clearly defined target of mental health. We know what we don't want but I'm unsure we have defined what we expect mental health to look like. If we don't have a target, we can't experience any real change.

If we don't know what success looks like how will we know when we've achieved it?

A successful method of achieving any change must have a positive approach.

The mind simply can't work with a negative instruction or target. It just can't be motivated to lose something that it has been programmed to maintain as 'normal'.

Here are two examples:

Dieting regimes are seldom successful over time. The concept of 'losing' weight is a negative and the mind is not conditioned to lose things. We are in a culture of gain so losing weight is a difficult target to achieve. However, creating a different body shape is a more positively focused target and so an exercise regime can be more successful in achieving the desired outcome.

The other example is if a young child has innocently picked up a dangerous object, such as a knife. How do we carefully persuade the child to give it up? To placate the child so we can remove the knife it's a proven strategy to swap the offending weapon with something less dangerous. Just taking the knife leaves the child with a loss which generally triggers a desire to get it back. By offering a safer alternative—a toy or candy—the child's attention is drawn away from the item you want to remove from them.

**Shifting Focus**

This shift of focus is vital in achieving change and it uses the mind's natural in-built motivations and strategies. These strategies work behind the scenes, as it were, at a level of consciousness that is beneath our moment-to-moment awareness, in something that has come to be known as the unconscious or subconscious.

So, referring to the list above and your own needs, consider again now what would be your personal, mental health positive outcomes?

If you haven't already done so, take a moment to write them down.

With regards to the Drop it! strategy, we will be working with the mind's primary drivers, not trying to change them but using them. As we learn to understand the mind, we take back control and practice using a specific gift that we have long forgotten how to use, to achieve our mental health goal.

That gift is our ability to think on purpose, the power to create thought rather than give our valuable attention and time to unwanted intrusive thoughts.

## Intrusive Thoughts

I want to focus a moment more here on intrusive thoughts, because this seems to be one of the biggest problems my clients want to overcome.

Intrusive thoughts are those thoughts which just come into our awareness without us thinking them. They tend to be negative. They can come like a flood. They can hang around and follow us throughout our day, despite our best efforts to clear our minds. I call it 'sticky thinking', and it influences our internal dialogue during the day and sometimes through the night as well.

Intrusive thoughts can be incredibly persuasive and, because we don't know what their source is, we can take them too seriously, just in case they contain information that might be relevant to our survival.

Consequently, we tend to hold on to intrusive thoughts even though they might be driving our feelings and our behaviour in a direction that is unhelpful or unwanted.

The basic human instinct of possession is a primary driver that we will be battling with if, for example, we ask the mind to drop an intrusive thought without replacing it with something else, something more useful, attractive, or pleasant.

Simply changing our mind or refocusing it doesn't seem to cut the mustard when it comes to managing our internal dialogue.

## Leave No Vacuum

We can't stop intrusive thoughts, that would be like removing our heart because we have high blood pressure or removing our brain because we don't want to think any more.

Humans are thinking creatures—it's part of our fallen nature to try to analyse and work out what's going on and find solutions to often self-created problems. So we need to understand as much as we can about the nature of how the unrenewed mind operates, how it creates and manages thought. It is, after all, our default human operating system from the day we are born until the day we die or are born again.

One key issue is that when we are training the mind to change the way it manages intrusive thoughts, we must leave no vacuum or empty space.

Without training, a vacuum in the mind will, naturally, be instantly filled with fresh intrusive thoughts just like a hole in the sand on a beach will be filled the next time the tide washes over it. The tide in our minds is the relentless flow of information to which we are exposed every waking moment of our lives.

We need a strategy that enables us to take control and equips us to feel confident that we are going to turn this around and begin to enjoy freedom and creativity within the personal space of our own minds.

Drop it! is such a strategy.

## A Professional's Struggle

When I was in my late twenties I suffered from stress, or, to put it more accurately, I was struggling with a compulsion that I needed to please other people which created stress.

The problem was that I didn't know how to please people. I'd been an only child and part of that upbringing was the perceived need to 'buy' friendships, so that I didn't feel lonely. I felt that I had to do what other kids wanted so they would like me.

My school reports didn't help and added more pressure; nearly every report informed my parents that I 'could do better' but I was never told what 'better' meant—an impossible target when I didn't know what was expected of me.

This followed through into my first job, estate agency. At my initial interview I was told that I had a nice smile. I was told that if I smiled, I would sell houses. Therefore, I pursued a career on the instructions that the more I smiled, the more houses I would sell, the more money I would earn, the more successful I would be. After a while my jaw ached.

These internal drivers then fed into my love relationships. Not so much the smiling perhaps, but the need to please, which became a compulsion to be compliant to the desires of my partner, to the degree that the other party in my relationships felt pressure to cope with a very needy partner.

I've spent most of my life looking for answers. Looking for solutions to the constant nagging sense that life could be better, easier, happier, more... relaxing!

I tried hypnosis. It seemed to work for a while and so I became a hypnotherapist so that I could not only maintain my own mental health but also help others find their own.

Hypnosis took me away from my relationship with God as I became more convinced that I was a god to the people I was trying to change. The more success, the more ego grabbed me by the lapels and dragged me into the world of manipulation and control.

So, I trained as a practitioner of the Three Principles of mind, consciousness and thought which, at the time, was being promoted as the new paradigm in psychology. But because my training was atheist, humanistic and based on life being a self-created illusion, it engendered in me a feeling of detachment, loss of self and I became morose and even more depressed.

Now that I've found peace with the principles as part of a practical model that aligns with the Bible, my love for life and people has returned and I want to give my time to helping others in psychological or spiritual darkness to find love and light.

So, the Drop it! method uses the mind's natural resources, and is also a pattern interruption strategy.

It can be instant and rewarding. It has given me control over my internal space. It makes every day an exciting experiment in living life to the full despite my external circumstances.

It brings me joy and peace, a sense of control, and inner contentment.

I enjoy my inner space and my sense of humour and it has enhanced my ability to cope and view life's mysterious ability to surprise and disappoint with a lightness that has been missing for years.

## Tackling the Issues

Let's examine three of the most common sources of mental ill health in our culture today (and in my own experience):

## Intrusive Thoughts

Why is it that our mind creates thoughts from nowhere, out of thin air, that annoy and worry us? Why is the unrenewed mind's default thought-feed negative?

There are many theories about this, mostly around natural protection and the need for survival but it's probably more likely our interpretation of the narrative.

Drop it! is about action, solution, freedom, and practice. Do this and you can be free from the effects of intrusive thoughts.

## The Thought/Feeling Connection

If we focus our attention on intrusive thoughts our body will begin to respond as the event cycle processes through the transition from thought to feelings. You know the way feelings follow thoughts? If we think about tomorrow's interview, we get nervous. If we think about yesterday's disastrous attempt at dating, we feel embarrassed. So wouldn't it be great to have the thought without the feeling?

In my opinion our mind-body system is supposed to work this way. We are supposed to have feelings that flow from our thinking. That's the way it works. We don't need to try to rewire a system that's been honed to perfection, probably over thousands of years. It's understanding the natural process that gives us power to influence it and when we see the inside-out revelation of God's Holy Spirit influencing our very private inner space, how can we not be humbled and mightily impressed at the same time!

Feelings are part of our make-up, but to de-link feelings from the thought source is like taking painkillers. If we don't feel the pain, how do we know we are injured and how will we know when we are healed?

Emotional pain works the same as physical pain—it's an indicator that something needs to be attended to.

As I said at the beginning, this method works with the way the mind-body system naturally works so we're not trying to change the way the system operates.

We work with the system but aim to recognise when we have let the old habits interfere with our relationship to the Holy Spirit's inspiration.

The mind will naturally fill a vacuum with intrusive thoughts.

## Mindfulness

Hours of meditation. Listening to experts through our earbuds, guiding us through a meditation that scans every inch of our body as we persuade ourselves to calm all these rebellious components— relaxing the toes, ankles, knees, thighs… try it without falling asleep from complete boredom!

I am a trained mindfulness practitioner. I have taught it to groups of highly intelligent engineering professionals. One mindfulness exercise is taking time to train our ability to pay close attention to detail, to reality as it presents itself to us, such as examining the sensory sensations of the look and taste of a raisin or piece of chocolate.

Mindfulness can bring peace and harmony, but it can also expose people to their deepest inner thoughts which, in terms of our fallen nature, can be disruptive if we are unprepared.

If our mind was naturally meant to be calm all the time, we wouldn't need to train it, would we? It's like if we were meant to live in water, we wouldn't need to learn how to swim, but we are land-dwelling creatures, and we have minds adapted to this lifestyle, to the degree that are incredibly capable of thinking at any level of stress and anxiety. We just don't work the system!

The mind is aware of everything that's going on around us, without us having to manage it and control it.

## Awareness is Useful Information

One of the mind's operating principles is observing or self-awareness, which we call consciousness or subconsciousness, but in Bible teaching is referred to as our Spirit.

For example, have you ever been driving your car when you realise you've not been concentrating? Maybe you've just spent a little too long glancing at someone on the footpath or at the scenery when suddenly your attention is snapped back to the flashing brake lights of the car in front, which has suddenly had to stop.

The mind thinks, that is what it does, that is what it is.

When we try to stop it thinking or try to refocus it on a candle flame or the leaf of a tree, we will find ourselves in an internal wrestling match as the mind floods us with intrusive thoughts about our health, relationships, and bank balance.

Remember, just as the tide naturally fills any holes in the sand with more sand, the mind naturally fills a vacuum in our thinking with more thoughts.

That's the way the system has been trained to work, so why do we try to change it? If we are super-aware of intrusive thoughts, we do not have a mental problem, we just need to recognise the thoughts that are spam, drop them, and move on, recognising that much of our habitual thinking is because there is an aspect of our system that it not yet fully renewed.

## Common Causes of Mental Distress

### 1. Disappointment

When working with clients I always ask them to identify why life keeps serving up disappointments. They often say things like, 'I expected to get the job, everything pointed to it from the interview, but the outcome was different and very disappointing,' or 'I really thought he liked me, but it turned out that he was already engaged to someone else, so that was really disappointing.'

To me, these scenarios indicate the difference between our personal imagination and fact.

Why do we trust our imagination to predict an outcome and then get disappointed when reality proves different? Surely, we should just accept reality as the default and move on, working with what has manifested and change that, just like in the burnt cakes metaphor.

Think about situations you have experienced where you have imagined outcomes that were proved incorrect by facts.

How did you deal with your feelings arising from disappointed thinking?

Do you still hold unresolved thoughts about any situations where facts proved your predictions to be wrong and you just can't let it go?

If we use the event cycle to drop from thinking to faith rather than feelings, God will direct our steps rather than having us take actions that arise from feelings.

'We make our plans, but the Lord determines our steps,' (Proverbs 16:9, NLT).

## 2. Projection

In our culture, the busy mind creates short cuts (which we call habits) to manage the amount of information it must process.

Our habits become personal preferences (just like the way we personalise the settings of our smartphone). It is because of these personal preferences that we view life from our perspective, then we tend to project these personal perspectives onto other people and of course we're surprised (and disappointed) when they don't match up.

The fact is that we all have different preferences so if we project ours onto other people two things happen—we will be disappointed when they don't match ours, and we won't give them the respect they deserve by listening to them, respecting their differences, and dropping our own expectations.

By dropping from thinking to faith we see what is really out there, not what we think is out there.

To quote Paul again, 'So, we don't look at the troubles we can see now; rather we fix our gaze on things that cannot be seen. For the things that we see now will soon be gone, but the things we cannot see will last forever,' (2 Corinthians 4:18, NLT).

## 3. Prejudgement

The third mental habit I've found operating in the background of unhappy clients is the tendency to anticipate how a situation or person is going to turn out and having that fixed opinion so firmly in their minds that they just don't see what is happening.

It's like we create a screen between us and the other person or the situation so that we are experiencing something that isn't as real as it could be. We are responding or reacting to our personally created version of life or people rather than what is happening.

## Moving the Mountains

Through our personal preferences, we create habitual thought-mountains.

Mountains of doubt, mountains of fear, mountains of sickness, mountains of depression and so on.

Many people have created in their personal minds an unassailable range of mountains, even snow-topped monster mountains that reach into the clouds of despair and the mists of uncertainty.

Ok, that's all very poetic but let's get back to facts. Do we need to move the mountain or do we need to scale the mountain, or do we need to conquer the mountain?

Well, no, because the mountain is built by us, constructed out of our own habits of thinking and experiences from our past and imaginations of a future yet to unfold.

Jesus said, 'I tell you the truth, you can say to this mountain, "May you be lifted up and thrown into the sea," and it will happen. But you must believe it will happen and have no doubt in your heart,' (Mark 11:23, NLT).

## Where Are You Now?

In terms of mental health management and solutions, this theory of 'now' has earned a lot of respect in the professional community. The concept of 'now' is proposed to bring us into focus with what is real and present rather than our imaginary future or memory-based past.

'Now' must be the answer to a quiet mind, surely? They tell us to 'be here now' or to 'live in the now'.

One little problem arises though. 'Now' can very quickly become 'then' because we are living in a culture where time has become a hugely influential factor in the way we experience life.

Time is accepted as a fact of life, but time has become one of the personal preferences that mean different things to different people. So, time is subjective and if subjective, then it can't be pinned down. Therefore, if time is not fixed it cannot therefore be used as a constant in the perfect mental health model that we all seek.

To be here now we can then think about the past without 'going there' and we can think about the future without going there. Our foundation, our grounding is strong.

As an illustration, think about how much time you spend in your memories and how much do they affect your present experience? Or how much time do you spend imagining a future and how does that affect your present experience?

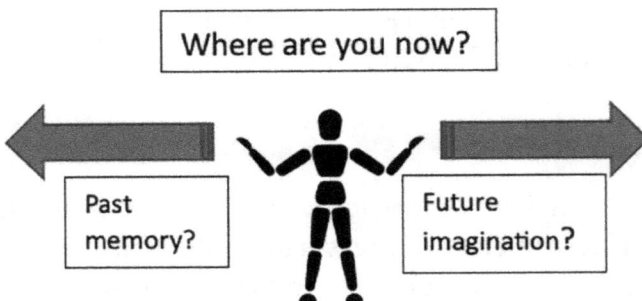

**Figure 17** Where Are You Now?

## Being now

I'm proposing a model, a method, an approach that gives you an influence over those intrusive thoughts without having to examine them, question them, reframe them, restructure them, or stick them in an imaginary bottle, pop in a cork, and throw them into an imaginary sea.

How you 'see' the model, how you imagine it, how you make it work for yourself is up to you. The method is nonprescriptive but the fundamental principles must be understood and acted upon.

The core idea must be undertaken exactly and must be practiced until you have confidence and control.

It's this simple: When an intrusive thought arises in your awareness, drop it.

Drop it like a hot potato, like a lump of manure that's fallen out of the sky into your cupped hands.

Drop it like it's carrying a virus, like it's radioactive.

How do you drop it?

You become unconscious of it.

In that moment, you go unconscious and switch your attention away from that thought.

It drops out of your awareness.
You drop it out of your awareness of that thought.

## Leave no Vacuum

If we fail to fill the vacuum a fresh intrusive thought will arise so we must have a replacement ready. This could be a favourite saying, or perhaps you have already prepared your go-to Bible quote, maybe 'For God so loved the world he gave his only

Son that whoever believes in is shall not perish but have eternal life.'

That's the Drop it!—interrupt, then concentrate on something else.

If you're awake and alert, you can concentrate on what's right in front of your eyes and fully engage with it, but if you're in bed, in the dark, you will probably have to work harder at constantly dropping intrusive thoughts and becoming unconscious to them.

Becoming unconscious to an intrusive thought doesn't mean that you become unconscious to everything around you. That is dangerous but we know that the mind is constantly aware of everything in your environment, so you can relax.

If you think on purpose, it's your choice if you want to drop that thought, but it doesn't make sense to think up something and then drop it—but that's up to you.

When you practice this, try dropping any thought. Don't be afraid. If the thought is worth having, it'll come back around.

Start with the first thought that intrudes your personal space.

Come on—you can own your personal space! It's your gift, this is your own space where you commune with God's Holy Spirit so why let anyone or anything else invade it?

Drop it.

Become unconscious to it. Something else will happen. It always does.

## The Creative Space Within

I would suggest that after about a week of dropping intrusive thoughts you will find that your creativity will increase. This is because you will have less clutter and be more able to think on purpose.

When you are ready, you can begin to use that space to create your mental model that is healthy for you, based in the renewed mind, with supernatural power and inspiration.

Until the barking dog is silenced it won't be easy to find comfort and rest.

Until we can experience rest, it isn't possible to unleash our true creative powers.

## Bringing the Target into Focus

So now you have space between the intrusive thoughts, and in that space, you can enjoy some peace, or you can create something new, because when you are beginning to create a new model for yourself, you will be laying down a new set of personal preferences, or habits.

The mind is now ready for continuous rebooting with some new, positive, purposeful thoughts that YOU want and that align with God's plan for you.

Maybe for the first time in your life you will realise that you have the privilege of being the co-operator of the most powerful creative force in the universe.

So, remember, if there's unwanted incoming? Drop it! Mental health in a moment!

# Chapter Seventeen

# Are You Giving Away Your Power?

## Introduction

*This is a new track on the album that is this book, metaphorically speaking. I wrote this chapter when yet another love relationship ended in heartbreak and I just thought what is going on, why do I keep falling for it?*

*By giving away my power to another human, either in love or business, I'm in danger of falling for the outside-in illusion that my happiness and wellbeing depends on them and consequently, the catch to this is that my wellbeing also depends on theirs and my life is then in danger and co-dependency becomes a potential issue. Their state of mind changes and mine doesn't, where does that leave me?*

*Compromise, compliance, adaptation, and the potential to lose my identity. So having learnt, eventually, to put myself first, so I'm not so needy, I can love and serve with less consequence.*

## The Outside-In Illusion

We derive pleasure from outside objects and events, but joy is something we develop on the inside.

If we decide that our happiness depends on our relationship with another person, when they decide they don't want to be part of the relationship anymore, we have given them the power to take our happiness with them.

If we derive our happiness from the greatest job in the world, our happiness will disappear with the job if it ends or we are made redundant.

If we are hoping and planning to have enough money to feel secure, we will consequently be discontent with what we have momentarily unable to fully enjoy the present moment, anticipating that more secure time in the future.

If we are fortunate enough then to secure that money our mind tends to switch to a different mode, one of protecting what we have. Now we might experience fear of losing the money because we have innocently programmed our mind that we must maintain that level of finance to ensure our ongoing sense of security.

The more we identify with an outside object, the more we will feel insecure because our mind will be working in the background to ensure that we are not going to be hurt. The mind becomes interdependent on the other person or activity or possession and will devise strategies to keep that option open. We become needy, putting unfair pressure on the other person.

The extreme outcome of this progressive dependency on something 'out there' leads to that other thing becoming our 'saviour', our life effectively only being secure when they or it complies to our needs and desires.

Self-sabotage can arise if we have experienced hurt or rejection in the past and our habitual thought pattern is we don't want to be hurt again. The mind will devise a different strategy and could well begin to push the object of desire away before it has the chance to pull away of its own accord.

This way the old mind's ego retains control and security, it retains the power it needs for security and dominance.

We can only become aware of this through the conscious state of the observer (spirit) when the mind's schemes are exposed.

The unrenewed mind will do its best to keep its strategies closed from the observing spirit, which is why we must persevere, not be afraid of what we might find, and not fear the emotions that might arise as we scan the mind's activities.

If adjustments need to be made in such a situation, go inside first because inside is where we have the power to change our settings.

You don't have to be the victim of the mind's strategic thought in the present moment.

Once we see that our present-moment experience can be contaminated by thoughts about the past we can drop into observer mode and take a subjective view of what's happening.

'But I don't like spending time with my memories because there is regret and hurt there.'

Memories are only thoughts in the moment, empowered by emotions that we have experienced in the past and are now being unconsciously linked to the present memory.

However, we cannot experience emotions from the past, they are only generated by thought in the moment.

We cannot easily remember something we haven't experienced. Can you remember all the thoughts you've ever had? No, we can only remember lived experiences that are logged in our memory and emotional circuits to help us navigate present times.

There is only now. Memories are past events reimagined in the present moment.

The future is a potential scenario imagined in the present moment.

To be present in the now, we need to accept that, in the vacuum of stillness, we will remember past, lived events and the body will mimic the feelings we had at the time we experienced them.

Once we become more spiritually aware and see that is what's happening, we can lean into the feelings rather than resisting them, and they will dissipate once the system realises that there is no real present threat, and the feelings are unnecessary.

The inside-out revelation is that the control room for manoeuvring in this particular mind strategy is in the observer mode.

To be free from the unrenewed mind's controlling safety-first strategy, we need to observe from beyond the mind, and that takes practice and honesty with ourselves first before we can be free from other-dependency and live truly in the present moment.

When living with the renewed mind, we drop out from thought to faith rather than feelings and in the space of faith we have the power of the Holy Spirit in any moment to receive peace and reassurance of our true identity and inheritance.

Our brain is a powerful bio-computer, but it cannot work on its own, it needs a power source, and that power source is God's spirit, producing thought and awareness.

God's spirit and the renewed mind provide all the resources we need to navigate life on planet earth.

Our personal, habitual mind works with the brain/body to create habitual thought that leads to habitual behaviours. If we leave the body alone, the operating system will continue to function in default mode. If we are driving home and become distracted by a phone call or radio programme, at the time we will become unconscious of the road, but our operating system will keep us driving unconsciously until we 'wake up' and ask ourselves, how did we get here?

Think about where you have given your power away, so you are no longer living in the moment, free from thoughts about the past or the future.

Have you given your power away to your partner, in either a love or work relationship?

Have you given your power away to an 'I'll be happy/secure/ contented when...' strategy?

Have you given your power away to a fantasy, alternative life that only exists in your mind?

The power to be present lays in really being present and seeing the truth that we are all made for companionship, but God has provided all we need to know him so that we don't become dependent on human love and give away our wellbeing and emotional control.

Isn't it enough that our spirit and the Holy Spirit are entwined and making beautiful music together in both the invisible heavenlies and the visible earth?

# Chapter Eighteen

# Practical Implications of the Cross

## Introduction

*In the 1980s, when I first became really interested in the life, death, and resurrection of Jesus Christ, I remember thinking about what implications this historical event had to do with me, personally. How could it be relevant to an ambitious, yet rather depressed, thirty-year-old in modern Britain?*

*I read C.S. Lewis's* Mere Christianity *and that had fascinated me, and then I'd come across a book by an American Church leader, Gordon MacDonald, called* Ordering Your Private World, *which appealed to my search for a deeper spiritual experience.*

*The God idea sounded appealing but organised religion and Church put me off. Also, my scepticism was strong at the time. It all seemed a bit too coincidental that an invisible God would materialise on earth and then become invisible again—that didn't make sense, especially as there didn't seem to be any real evidence of his influence, what with the amount of death, wars, earthquakes, corruption, and so on.*

*It also seemed to be too much of a handy coincidence that the evidence for Jesus was primarily in God-biased materials such as the Bible. I needed to find lived experience of people who had really been changed by their faith in this invisible God.*

*Encouraged by my enquiries, a Christian friend told me that nobody would ever be able to 'see' God until they died and although that made sense at the time, I just fell into that cosy mindset of beliefs that if I went to church and did good stuff then one day, when I died, I would meet God and then be able to ask him personally why the world was such a mess.*

*It was during another conversation with my 'die to meet God' friend that the implications of what he actually meant dawned on me. He meant that we don't have to wait until we physically die to know God but there is a part of us that blocks our ability to see God at all, let alone in person. To put it personally, my earthbound rebellious ego self is so self-absorbed, critical, and influenced by the world that I'm blinded to the influence of God in the world and that is the part of me that has to be put to death now, in this life, before I physically die.*

*'You must be born again,' my friend advised. 'You cannot see the Kingdom of God unless you die to your old self-centred ways and are born again.*

*I'd heard about being born again, but I'd never considered that involved death too!*

*'So how do I die?' I asked.*

*'By faith,' he answered.*

*Oh, here we go again, I thought, more invisible shenanigans. Why doesn't God just show up and shake hands with me!*

*My friend went on. 'God wants you to be his representative on Earth, he doesn't want you to die physically but he wants to eliminate your sinful nature. Your old operating system must die so he can install the new system.'*

*'How does this happen?'*

*'The cross is where the death happens, and a time called Pentecost is when the new system is installed.'*

*I must admit I was a bit lost now. I was still thinking that this was all a bit far-fetched!*

*The things is, if we look to the Bible as having any practical value for life then its far-fetched story of death and renewal should be taken more seriously. Why wasn't this more widely known, after all, the Bible has been top of the bestseller list for longer than any other book ever written.*

*So, I now come to the point in this book where the cross of Christ cannot be ignored.*

## Sacrifice

My search for inner peace has led me on a psycho–spiritual journey into a deeper aspect of the human condition, but if I follow the logic that my habitual mind is infected by a legacy of insecurity and fear, I cannot change it myself nor can I save myself from the curse of death that comes with ancestral rebellion. I now turn to God's ultimate sacrifice which is his initiative to save us rebellious sinners from ourselves and bring us into the Kingdom of his love.

The Passion Translation of the New Testament, John 19:30, tells of Jesus's final words from the cross: 'When he had sipped the sour wine, he said, "It is finished, my bride," then he bowed his head and surrendered his spirit to God.' (TPT).

There are many references in the Bible to the Church being the 'bride of Christ' and that he has chosen the Church as his lover, his representative on earth waiting for his return, loving the world though a turbulent time in between his first and last manifestations.

The work of salvation was finished on the cross, at the moment he gave up his spirit and his physical mission ended, but what began was the release of all those who had died before, the release from the grip of death, risen, resurrected with him to a new type of life, part of the new creation.

In Matthew's Gospel is an account of the moment that Jesus gave up his spirit: 'At that moment the curtain in the sanctuary was torn in two from top to bottom. The earth shook, rocks split apart, and tombs opened. The bodies of many Godly men and women who had died were raised from the dead. They left the cemetery after Jesus's resurrection, went into the holy city of Jerusalem and appeared to many people,' (Matthew 27:51, NLT).

What are the practical implications of this historic event that shook the earth and caused people to rise from their graves?

What does salvation mean for us now, today, in our search for inner peace and the meaning of life?

## The Cross for Today

Have you ever thought when life is really getting sticky, 'I wish I could start again.'?

The cross enables us to start again.

In the moment of his death, he was like a divine/human-hybrid black hole, powered by God to suck all the sickness of the fallen world into himself.

The consequence of rebellion is death, and he took the place of the rebel called Barabbas who should have died on that cross.

Instead, the people chose Jesus as the one who should die but by doing that, they pressed the 'go' button for the completion of God's plan of redemption and healing.

All of the consequences of the fall of humanity in the Garden of Eden, such as being cast out into the wilderness, sickness, pain, mental and emotional confusion, death, and decay were sucked out of all those sufferers and into the human body of Jesus Christ and it killed him, exposed and naked, bloodied, and forsaken.

Everything we are struggling with today was taken away in Jesus on the cross, then taken and laid in a cave for three days while everything was restored, and God raised Jesus to new life as the first of a new breed of hybrid humans.

So, we need to take the suffering we still experience as the legacy of being born through the blood line of Adam to the cross for God to release us, one by one by one.

## The Cross and the Event Cycle

The event of the cross was for all eternity, so we use it today as the antidote to the crisis facing humanity.

The event was Jesus's crucifixion.

Our personal thoughts arising from the event will determine our fate.

If our thoughts are in line with God's plan, we will feel that we are saved by his love and the sacrifice of Jesus.

Thoughts of fear will turn to thoughts of faith.

Thoughts of mental confusion will turn to hope and purpose.

Our feelings arising from the thoughts will be reset from isolation to adoption, from confusion to wonder, from outside striving to inside contentment.

The actions arising from feelings will be motivated by love, peace, and security.

We are already home, and now we can step back out into the world as fishers of a broken humanity, still pulling the lost from the rapids one by one, but our mission will be more informed because we will know what's causing them to be in the water in the first place.

The cross is a subject that is far too broad and expansive to give justice to in this book. Please explore this more through the Bible and if possible one-to-one Bible study with a qualified minister of the Word of God.

# Conclusion

## Two Routes, One Destination

Love can be a difficult emotion and as a coping mechanism I have sometimes rationalised and projected it, taking out the personal emotion and looking at how to act *in* love rather than *out* of love.

In love, I want everyone I meet to know God, humanity's creator, through Jesus, and for everyone to enjoy a personal relationship with the Holy Spirit. In this inside-out experience, the eternal life that God's Kingdom offers has all the resources that are lacking in the humanistic earthbound experience.

In love, I want people who decide that the biblical God experience is not for them to be able to enjoy their time on planet earth with the best peace of mind and contentment, manifesting their passion for life through their jobs or relationships.

For this reason, understanding the inside-out nature of the Three Principles of mind, consciousness, and thought can break the patterns of the world and it is my hope that the 'spiritual' nature of these psychological principles will begin to heal humanity's broken communication with God the creator too.

The heart of God is for all creation to know and love and he reaches out constantly to all of us, healing not only each individual but restoring the nations of the world that are in conflict, bringing one love through the spirit of his son Jesus Christ.

God has revealed the psychological principles to help us heal our minds and restore the nations to order but that is just the beginning. Through restoring the communion between earth and heaven we each become new creatures, a new humanity with the promise of a new earth, Eden restored.

I believe that the Three Principles understanding, when seen in a biblical context, can help in healing the rift between human psychology and the spiritual church.

There is an old saying about getting to the heart of a matter that asks, are we just moving the deckchairs on the Titanic?

Well, if principles-based psychology enables us to move the deckchairs of our minds, it's God's Church that knows where those deckchairs should be best placed to catch the rays from the sun.

# Annexe

# My Old Amplified New Testament

## Introduction

*When I was researching my notes from the past fifteen years, I discovered an old Amplified Bible New Testament. As I'm an explorer of the meaning of life my first Bible as a new Christian was a Good News New Testament. Written in simple language, it was a paraphrase, in other words not a word-for-word translation, but an easy-to-understand guide to God's plan for human redemption.*

*Back then, I needed to study scripture more deeply and amongst other translations, there was the Amplified Bible, it added a sort of commentary within the text, but more than that, in tiny writing, in the covers, were my notes from the early Church days that were important to understanding how to live the Christian life.*

*I've reproduced those notes here because on re-reading them I've found a treasure trove of scripture references which I thought you might find useful if this book has inspired you to explore the Christian life more deeply, and what it means practically to enjoy the inside-out revelation.*

## The Christian Described

A sinner saved by grace: Acts 11:26, Ephesians 1:8, 1 Timothy 1:15

A member of God's family: Romans 9:15, John 1:12, Ephesians 3:14

A disciple of Jesus Christ: Luke 14:26, Matthew 9:9

A temple of the Holy Spirit: Acts 7:48, 1 Corinthians 6:19

A pilgrim in an alien environment: Hebrews 11:8, 1 Peter 2:11

## The Christian Life

A vocation to be fulfilled: Philippians 3:14, Romans 15:20, Colossians 1:18
A character to be developed: Romans 8:29, 2 Peter 1:15, Ephesians 5:1
A fellowship to be maintained: 1 John 1:1, Ephesians 4:3, John 15:4
Energies to be harnessed: 1 Corinthians 15:58, Ephesians 2:10, Colossians 3:23
Minds to be developed: 1 John 15:20, Ephesians 4:13, Ephesians 1:18
A hope to be realised: 1 Peter: 1:3, Titus 2:13, Revelation 22:20

## The Christian and the World

Called out of the world: 1 Corinthians 7:29, Hebrews 10:33, Colossians 3:1
Separated from the world: James 4:4, Ephesians 5:3, John 17:15
To overcome the world: Romans 8:19, Ephesians 6:10, Romans 8:37
To journey through the world: Philippians 3:20, Hebrews 11:16
Sent into the world: John 20:21, Matthew 5:15, John 3:16

## The Christian and the Bible

Directs the Christian for life: John 8:31, Matthew 7:24
Equips the Christian for battle: Matthew 4:1, 1 Timothy 1:18, Ephesians 6:17
Energises the Christian for service: John 15:16
Corrects the Christian from error: Mark 7:9, James 1:23
Develops the Christian in the faith: 2 Timothy 2:15, 1 Corinthians 14:20, 1 Peter 2:2
Informs the Christian of God's mind: Romans 11:33, 2 Timothy 3:14

## The Christian and Prayer

For communion with God: Matthew 6:5, Mark 1:35, Luke 5:15
For growth in God: Ephesians 3:14, Matthew 6:9
For the service of God: 1 Thessalonians 5:16
For experience of God: Acts 16:22, 2 Corinthians 12:7

## The Christian and Witness

Proclaiming a person: Acts 1:8, Acts 8:35, Luke 24:46
Explaining the truth: Colossians 1:28, Acts 18:4, 2 Timothy 2:2
Sharing a love: 2 Corinthians 5:14, 1 Thessalonians 2:7
Witnessing consistently: John 13:34, Philippians 2:14, 1 Peter 3:15
Witnessing personally: Acts 4:18, Acts 8:1 and 4
Witnessing collectively: Acts 2:14, Acts 42:47, Philippians 1:27

# Copyrights, Sources & Acknowledgements

## Scripture Quotations

### *New International Version*

Scripture quotations marked (NIV) are taken from The Holy Bible, New International Version (Anglicised edition) copyright © 1979, 1984, 2011 by Biblica (formerly International Bible Society), used by permission of Hodder and Stoughton Publishers, a Hachette UK company. All rights reserved. 'NIV' is a registered trademark of Biblica (formerly International Bible Society) UK trademark number 1448790.

### *English Standard Version®*

Scripture quotations marked (ESV) are from the ESV® Bible (The Holy Bible, English Standard Version®), Copyright © 2001 by Crossway, a publishing ministry of Good News Publishers. Used by permission. All rights reserved. The 'ESV' and 'English Standard Version' are registered trademarks of Crossway, use of each trademark requires the permission of Crossway.

### *The Passion Translation©*

Scripture quotations marked (TPT) are from The Passion Translation®. Copyright © 2017, 2018 by Passion & Fire Ministries, Inc. Used by permission. All rights reserved. ThePassionTranslation.com.

### *New Living Translation*

Scripture quotations market (NLT) are taken from The Holy Bible New Living Translation Copyright © 1996. Used by permission of Tyndale House Publishers Inc. Wheaton, Illinois 60189 United States of America. All rights Reserved.

*In-perception®*

In-perception® is a trademark of David Robert Cotterill UK 00003040208 and should not be used in any form of media, promotions, therapy, coaching, psychology, or education without the express written permission of David Robert Cotterill. All rights reserved.

**The Event Cycle, Conscious Levels and the Overthinking Progression** are copyright David R Cotterill. All rights reserved.

*The Three Principles Global Community (3PGC)*

The Three Principles Global Community (3PGC) is a non-profit organization committed to disseminating the understanding of the Three Principles, as discovered by Sydney Banks, to people throughout the world. The Three Principles point toward the true source of human experience. Insightful realization of the Three Principles allows anyone to understand how all human experience is created, and to glimpse the very nature of that creative source. These insights uncover our natural resilience, innate feelings of wellbeing, and our natural connection and access to a universal wisdom found within everyone.
https://3pgc.org/

**David R Cotterill** can be contacted through Mentoringforlife. co.uk

www.ingramcontent.com/pod-product-compliance
Lightning Source LLC
Chambersburg PA
CBHW031146270326
41931CB00006B/155